Buying &
Selling
your
House

If you want to know how...

Making Money from Letting
How to buy and let residential property for profit

Save Thousands Buying Your Home
*A step-by-step guide to reducing the price of a house
and the cost of your mortgage*

Buy to Let Property Hotspots
Where to buy property and how to let it for profit

Property Hotspots in London
Where in our capital city to buy and let property for profit

How to Get on the Property Ladder
*The first-time buyer's guide to escaping the rent trap
and owning your own home*

howtobooks

Please send for a free copy of the latest catalogue:

How To Books
3 Newtec Place, Magdalen Road,
Oxford OX4 1RE, United Kingdom
email: info@howtobooks.co.uk
http://www.howtobooks.co.uk

Buying & Selling your House

Adam Walker

howtobooks

Published by
How To Books Ltd, 3 Newtec Place
Magdalen Road, Oxford OX4 1RE. United Kingdom.
Tel: (01865) 793806. Fax: (01865) 248780.
email: info@howtobooks.co.uk
http://www.howtobooks.co.uk

First edition 2004

British Library Cataloguing in Publication Data
A catalogue record for this book is available from the British
Library

Produced for How To Books by Deer Park Productions,
Tavistock
Typeset by PDQ Typesetting, Newcastle-under-Lyme, Staffs.
Cover design by Baseline Arts Ltd, Oxford
Printed and bound by Cromwell Press Ltd, Trowbridge, Wiltshire

NOTE: The material contained in this book is set out in good
faith for general guidance and no liability can be accepted
for loss or expense incurred as a result of relying in particular
circumstances on statements made in the book. The laws and
regulations are complex and liable to change, and readers should
check the current position with the relevant authorities before
making personal arrangements.

Contents

List of illustrations

Preface

This book is a thoroughly practical guide to buying and selling a house or flat. If you are buying a property this book will guide you step by step through the whole process and help to ensure that you buy the right property in the right area at the right price. If you are selling a property this book will help to ensure that you achieve a quick and trouble-free sale at the very best possible price.

IMPENDING LEGISLATION

The government is intending to make radical changes to the house-buying process. It intends to bring in new legislation which, from January 2006, will make it a criminal offence to market a property without first preparing a seller's information pack. If this legislation is introduced, it will alter the house-buying process fundamentally. However, the legislation has already been postponed once and at the time of writing it is still unclear whether it will ever be introduced. If it is, we will immediately bring out a new edition of this book. In the meanwhile the likely effects of the new legislation are considered in detail in Chapter 23.

The advice contained in this book is based on the feedback from more than 100,000 property professionals who have attended my training courses and seminars during the last 17 years. I am very grateful to them for their input. Thanks also go to my secretary Lyn Harding for her patience, good humour and attention to detail during each draft of this book.

Adam Walker

Part One
Buying A House

(1)

Buying Versus Renting

I shall start by asking the most important question in the whole of this book.

Are you absolutely certain that you want to buy a property at this time?

Many people who became home owners during the 1980s did so because there was no viable alternative. The result of draconian anti-landlord legislation passed in 1977, was that there were few privately owned properties available to rent during the 1980s. This left most people with a choice between joining a long waiting list to rent a council or housing association owned property, or buying their own home. The consequence was that by 1988 home ownership levels in the United Kingdom had risen to almost 70%, one of the highest rates in the developed world.

Today the situation is completely different. The Housing Act, which was passed in 1988, made letting a property a much more attractive proposition for landlords and today there is a plentiful supply of good quality privately owned property available to rent in most areas. Before you commit yourself to buying a property, you would do well to reconsider the alternative of renting somewhere.

KEY ADVANTAGES OF RENTING A PROPERTY

Flexibility

The most important advantage of rented property is its flexibility. Most tenancies are of six or twelve months duration. At the end of this period you can walk away without any further cost or obligation. If your future plans are uncertain, you may find that renting a property is a much better bet.

Speed

It is usually possible to move into a rented property within a few days of seeing it. Buying a property usually takes three to four months. If you are in a hurry to move, a rented property might be a useful stopgap.

Convenience

Repairs and maintenance are usually the responsibility of the landlord. This could be important if you work very long hours or don't have the inclination to undertake or supervise day-to-day repairs. It also makes it easier to plan your budget accurately.

KEY ADVANTAGES OF OWNING A PROPERTY

Capital growth

If you rent a property for 25 years, you will end up with nothing. If you buy the property on a 25-year mortgage, you will, at the end of the mortgage term, own it outright. The opportunity to achieve a capital gain in this way is, for many home owners, the single most important factor behind their decision to buy their own property.

Cost

In the long term buying a property will probably cost less than renting one. At the time of writing most commercial landlords are aiming to achieve a gross yield of around 9% from their investment. This means that the owner of a property worth £100,000 will be hoping to achieve an annual rental of £100,000 × 9%, i.e. £9,000 per annum. Out of this the landlord will have to pay for repairs and maintenance and also, in most cases, a fee to the managing agents.

If you were to borrow money at say 6% to buy a similar property your mortgage would be £100,000 × 6%, i.e. £6,000 per annum.[1] This gives a gross saving of £3,000 per annum out of which the cost of repairs and maintenance will have to be met.

Taking everything into account, it is usually cheaper to own a property than to rent one. However, this is not always the case as average yields do vary significantly from property to property and from area to area. (Generally speaking landlords of cheaper properties expect to achieve higher yields than landlords of larger and/or more expensive properties.)

Another factor to take into account is the costs associated with buying and reselling a property. If you expect to stay in the property for less than two years it would probably be cheaper to rent than to buy.

---

1   Due to the way that mortgage interest payments are calculated the true annual percentage rate of the loan may be higher than 6% and the payments increased accordingly.

NON-FINANCIAL FACTORS TO CONSIDER

In addition to the financial arguments there are some important emotional factors to consider.

The disruption of repeated moves

Many rented properties are only available for a fixed term. If you chose to rent a property, you are far more likely to have to face the stress and disruption of further moves.

Decoration

You will not usually be allowed to change the decor of a rented property. Many people find that they cannot feel truly at home until they have decorated to their own taste.

Care of furnishings

Most furnished properties come with carpets and curtains and many are fully or partly furnished. The need to be constantly careful to protect someone else's furnishings prevents many people from feeling fully at home in a rented property.

FINDING A PROPERTY TO RENT

Lettings/Property management agents

In most areas there are one or more estate agents who specialise in rented property. Their service is free to prospective tenants so it is well worth registering your requirements with all the firms in the local area.

The agents will probably start by asking you some questions to ensure that you are a suitable prospective tenant. If you give the right answers, you will probably be told about suitable properties over the telephone and encouraged to view immediately. Property management is a very fast moving business and properties often come and go within a few hours. Because of this many agents do not prepare written particulars of the properties that are available for rent. Your decision to view will therefore usually have to be made on the basis of a phone call.

Agreeing the rent

Rents for apparently identical properties can vary enormously so it is well worth shopping around by registering with more than one agent. Rents are often negotiable, so when you find somewhere that you like it is worth trying an offer – you can always increase it if the landlord says no.

References

Landlords fear two things:

◆ That you will not pay the rent.
◆ That you will damage their property.

In order to protect themselves from these threats, most landlords will ask for financial, employment and personal references.

Tenancy agreements

Most tenancy agreements are now 'assured short hold tenancies'. The essence of the agreement is that you commit to pay the agreed rent for the agreed period and the landlord guarantees you the right to occupy the property for the whole of the agreed term – usually six or twelve months.

Deposits

Most landlords will require a deposit of at least one month's rent. The cost of any damage to the property will be deducted from this at the end of the term.

The failure to return deposits is a very common cause of disputes between landlords and tenants. The best way to safeguard your deposit is to arrange the tenancy through a reputable agent who can act as mediator in any future dispute. Most reputable lettings agents are members of the Association of Residential Letting Agents (ARLA). ARLA has strict rules over the handling of deposits by its members.

Checking in

Another precaution that you should take to safeguard your deposit is to make a careful inspection of the condition of the property at the start of the tenancy. Any damage should be pointed out to the landlord or the managing agent, recorded in writing and, if possible, photographed.

SUMMARY

Financially it is usually better to buy a property than to rent one. However you should consider renting a property if:

- ◆ You are planning to move again in less than two years.
- ◆ You are moving to an unfamiliar area.
- ◆ You need to move very quickly.
- ◆ You do not have the time or inclination to deal with day-to-day maintenance and repairs.
- ◆ You are unsure of your future plans.

Case study

David M was asked to move from Yorkshire to west London by his employer. He and his wife Karen spent a whole week looking for a property to buy. Prices in west London were far higher than they were in Yorkshire and it quickly became clear that they would have to make some compromises. After looking at more than 40 houses in six days they bought a house in a village about ten miles west of his new office at Heathrow. Within days of moving in they regretted their decision. The village, which had seemed quite pleasant during the day, was full of rowdy teenagers during the evenings. The journey to work took much longer than David had expected – an hour and five minutes to do ten miles. Worst of all the headmaster of their daughter's new primary school was unable to recommend any good secondary school in the area.

After a thoroughly unhappy first year they sold up and moved to a smaller house in a much nicer village five miles away.

Commenting on his experience David said 'we bought the first house in far too much of a hurry. With hindsight I wish that we had rented somewhere for the first six months and got to know the area properly. The extra move has cost us thousands of pounds and caused a great deal of unnecessary stress and frustration.'

Case study

Philip B moved from Manchester to east London with his job. The job move came up at short notice and Philip rented a two-bedroom flat in the Docklands area because he did not have time to look for somewhere to buy.

Philip liked the flat so much that he extended the initial twelve-month tenancy three times. After four years in the flat Philip's landlord gave him notice that he had decided to sell it. This prompted Philip to start looking for property to buy. When he started looking, he was horrified to find that prices had risen dramatically in the intervening four years.

Commenting on his experience Philip said 'with hindsight I should have bought my own property years ago – as soon as it became apparent that I was going to stay in the London area. As a result of my dithering I have ended up paying much more than I needed to for my new home.'

(2)

Understanding the Process

The process for buying a property in England and Wales is horribly inefficient. The average time between an offer being accepted and completion is 12 weeks. This is twice as long as it takes it most other countries. Worse still one third of all the sales that are agreed fail to reach completion. When a sale does fall through, buyers can be left with a bill for abortive costs of several thousand pounds.

The Government has said that it intends to change the home-buying process. From January 2006 it will become a criminal offence to market a property without first preparing a seller's information pack. The consequences of this will be very far-reaching and are discussed in detail later in this book. However, until January 2006 the house-buying process will continue to work in much the same way as it has done for the last 300 years.

In view of this I will start this chapter by explaining the current home-buying process. By gaining a better under-standing of the process you will be able to avoid many of the most common pitfalls.

THE ROLE OF THE ESTATE AGENT

A survey found that estate agents are less popular than used-car salesmen, double glazing salesmen and even politicians. People love to hate their estate agent but much of this antipathy arises because of a widespread mis-understanding of the estate agent's role.

An estate agent has a commercial, ethical and legal duty to work on behalf of his client, i.e. the vendor. This means getting the best price for the property, negotiating terms that are favourable to the vendor and acting in accordance with the vendor's instructions at all times.

As the purchaser, you should expect estate agents to be helpful and friendly towards you in order to encourage you to view the properties that they have available. But, however nice the estate agent is, you must never forget that his job is to act in the interests of the other side.

The estate agent's main functions during the sale are to:

- Advise the vendor on the optimum asking price for the property.

- Prepare sales particulars and check their accuracy.

- Send particulars to all potential buyers on the mailing list.

- Follow up the particulars with a phone call in order to maintain the maximum number of viewings.

- Encourage interested purchasers to make an offer.

- Negotiate on the vendor's behalf to achieve the highest possible price.

- Qualify the buyer to make sure that they are in a position to proceed immediately with their purchase.

◆ (Sometimes) arrange mortgage finance on behalf of the buyer.

◆ Liaise with the purchaser, mortgage lender and both solicitors on a regular basis to ensure that the sale is proceeding smoothly.

THE ROLE OF THE MORTGAGE LENDER

Most building societies were set up during Victorian times. When they were originally set up, they were mutual organisations owned by their members and their objectives were largely altruistic. They paid a fair rate of interest to attract savers and used this money to help ordinary working people to buy their own homes. A hundred years ago very few people had any savings and building societies were the only possible source of mortgage funding for most would-be home buyers.

Today the situation is entirely different. Banks, insurance companies and specialised mortgage lenders all compete with the traditional building societies to lend money in the mortgage market. Mortgage money is in plentiful supply and building societies are wholly commercial organisations. Today mortgage money is simply another commodity.

The importance of shopping around to obtain the most competitive mortgage rate is explained in detail in Chapter 4.

THE ROLE OF THE SURVEYOR

The surveyor's role is often widely misunderstood. Many people mistakenly believe that the survey will point out

any defects that the property has and confirm its market
value. The surveyor will not do this unless he is paid an
additional fee to do so.

About 80% of all house buyers opt for the most basic
form of survey, the mortgage valuation. A mortgage
valuation is exactly what is says it is. The surveyor acts for
his client, i.e. the mortgage lender, and answers just one
question. Is the property satisfactory security for the loan
that is being advanced?

If you want to know more about the condition of the
property, you will need to instruct the surveyor to
undertake a home-buyer's report or a building survey.
The various pros and cons of the different types of survey
that are available are explained in detail in Chapter 9.

THE ROLE OF YOUR SOLICITOR

Your solicitor's job is to safeguard your legal interest and
the interests of your mortgage lender (if any). Their main
functions are as follows:

Receives/Negotiates draft contract

Your solicitor will check the contract prepared by the
vendor's solicitors and amend any clauses which he feels
are detrimental to your interests.

Sends local search to council

A local authority search verifies, amongst other things,
whether the road is a private road (in which case you may
have to pay for its maintenance), whether the property
could be affected by any road widening schemes and
whether the property is in a conservation area. Some local

authorities take several weeks to deal with search enquiries and it is therefore important to apply for the search as soon as the sale has been agreed.

Sends preliminary enquiries to vendor's solicitor

This is a list of questions about the property. It will include questions such as 'does the property have mains drainage' and 'have there been any disputes over boundaries and fences'. Most of the questions are fairly standard and most solicitors use a standard word processed form with supplementary questions added as necessary.

Checks mortgage offer

Before exchanging contracts your solicitor will check that your mortgage offer is in order and that you are able to comply with all its terms and conditions.

Arranges signing of contract

Once your solicitor is happy with the terms of the contract he will ask you to sign it. At this point he will need your deposit (usually 10% of the purchase price).

Exchanges contracts

Your solicitor should not exchange contracts until he is happy with the terms of the contract, the results of the searches and absolutely certain that your mortgage and other funding is in place. Once you have exchanged contracts the sale is binding. If you withdraw now, you will forfeit your deposit. The vendor may also sue you for additional damages.

Checks vendor's title

The vendor's solicitor will have sent your solicitor proof of title in the form of a copy of the Title Deeds or a summary of their contents (known as an Abstract Title). If your solicitor has any questions, he will ask for clarification in writing. This correspondence is known as 'Requisitions on Title'.

Checks mortgage arrangements

Your solicitor will inform your mortgage lender of the completion date and ask them to ensure that the necessary mortgage funds are available on that date. He will also arrange for you to sign the mortgage deed and the conveyance or transfer document (see next paragraph).

Prepares draft conveyance or transfer

Your solicitor will prepare a draft transfer if the land is registered, or a conveyance if the land is unregistered (see later). This is the deed which will pass the vendor's interest in the property to you. This draft conveyance or transfer will then be sent to the vendor's solicitor so that he can check that it is in accordance with the terms of the contract.

Arranging signing of final documents

These will include the final (known as the engrossed) version of the conveyance or transfer and the mortgage deed. You will also at this time need to give your solicitor a cheque for the balance of any purchase monies required which are not to be paid out of your mortgage advance.

Commissions final searches

Your solicitor will carry out two final searches before completion. A bankruptcy search will confirm that the vendor is not bankrupt. If he is, the property might no longer be his to sell. The second and final search is a land charges search. This will ensure that there are no undisclosed mortgages or other charges against the property.

Arranges payment of Stamp Duty

If the purchase price was more than £60,000, the conveyance or transfer has to be sent to the Inland Revenue. A tax known as Stamp Duty is payable on all transactions over £60,000. At the time of writing this is payable according to the following scale:

£60,001 – £250,000 Stamp Duty payable at 1%
£250,001 – £500,000 Stamp Duty payable at 3%
£500,001 and above Stamp Duty payable at 4%

Arranges registration of title

Your solicitor's penultimate job is to register your title with the Land Registry. If you bought the property in joint names, all owners will be registered in the Proprietorship Register. Details of your mortgage and other charges will also be included in the Charges Register.

Deals with charges certificate

Once your title has been registered, the Land Registry will send a Charge Certificate to your solicitor. This confirms that the Land Registry has recorded the charge against the property. Your solicitor will forward the Charge Certificate to your mortgage lender.

If no mortgage is involved, the Land Registry will send your solicitor a Land Certificate. This proves that you own the property outright. It is an extremely important document and it is important to keep it in a safe place (most people entrust it to their bank).

THE ROLE OF THE VENDOR'S SOLICITOR

The vendor's solicitor is on the vendor's side. Their job is to provide your solicitor with the information that is requested and protect their client's legal interests during the course of the sale. Their main functions during the sale are as follows:

Obtains the Title Deeds

The Title Deeds are the documents that prove that the vendor actually owns the property that he is selling to you. If the property is mortgaged, they will usually be held by the mortgagee. In most cases obtaining the Title Deeds will take seven to ten days.

Orders office copy entries

If the property is registered (see later), the vendor's solicitor will apply to the Land Registry for office copy entries of the title. The office copy entries prove that the property is registered. They also give details of mortgages or other charges secured on the property and include a plan showing the extent of the land that is being sold.

If the property is 'unregistered' (see later) a Public Index Map Search is carried out to obtain proof of ownership.

Prepares draft contract
This is the document that sets out all the terms of the sale. It will be sent to your solicitor for approval.

Answers preliminary enquiries
Your solicitor will ask a number of questions about the property. These will include questions such as 'Is the property connected to mains drainage?' and 'Have there ever been any disputes over boundaries or fences?'. The vendor's solicitor is obliged to answer these questions truthfully. However, in practice many of the answers will be qualified with phrases such as 'as far as the seller is aware' or 'to the best of our knowledge'.

Prepares engrossed contract
This is the final version of the contract which will be signed by both parties.

Arranges for the vendor to sign the contract
If the property is jointly owned, all parties will need to sign.

Receives the deposit on exchange of contracts
This is usually 10% of the purchase price but a lesser figure is sometimes negotiated. Once contracts have been exchanged, the sale becomes binding on both parties and failure to complete could lead to the forfeiture of this deposit.

Sends evidence of title to the purchaser's solicitor
Once contracts have been exchanged, the vendor's solicitor will send your solicitor a copy of the Deeds or a summary of their contents (known as an abstract of title).

Discharges mortgages

The vendor's solicitor will ask the vendor's building society for a final settlement and ensure that the mortgage is paid out of the proceeds of the sale.

Arranges signing of final documents

The vendor's solicitor will check that the transfer or conveyance (see page 98) is in accordance with the terms of the contract before the vendor signs the final documents.

Arranges completion

The vendor's solicitor will receive the balance of the purchase monies and in return will hand over the Title Deeds to your solicitor.

Arranges the removal of charges

If the vendor had a mortgage on the property, this will be registered at the Land Registry. If this is the case, the vendor's solicitor must deduct the sum owing from the proceeds of the sale and send it, together with the mortgage form (known as Form 53) to the mortgage lender. The mortgage lender will officially stamp the form to confirm that the mortgage has been paid and return it to the vendor's solicitors. He will forward the form to your solicitor and your solicitor will forward it to the Land Registry.

BUYING A PROPERTY WITH UNREGISTERED TITLE

There are two systems of land conveyancing in England and Wales, Registered Title and Unregistered Title. In the first case the title to the land is registered at the Land Registry and guaranteed by the state. Disputes over title are therefore extremely rare. In the unregistered system title must be proved by checking back through details of previous conveyances. Where land is unregistered, disputes over title are much more common and can take a considerable time to resolve.

One day all land in England and Wales will be registered. In the meanwhile, if you find that the property that you are buying does not have registered title you should be prepared to allow extra time for the conveyancing process to be completed. You will also probably find that the conveyancing costs are significantly higher.

BUYING A LEASEHOLD PROPERTY

A freehold property is yours forever. A leasehold property is owned by a 'freeholder' who grants you the right to live there for a certain period of time. Most new leases are for a duration of 99 or sometimes 999 years, although in some areas, particularly central London, they are often much shorter.

The pros and cons of buying a leasehold property are discussed in Chapter 5.

If you do decide to buy a leasehold property, your solicitor will have to make two further checks.

Check the terms of the lease

The lease is a lengthy document that sets out amongst other things, who is responsible for maintaining the building and any restrictions that are imposed on the owners (for example not to keep a pet animal). Your solicitor will read the lease carefully to check that it does not contain any clauses that are detrimental to your interests. Some of the problems that are found with leases are explained in Chapter 11.

Check that service charges and grounds rents have been paid

The service charge reflects each leaseholder's share of the cost of maintaining the building. The ground rent is a (usually) small rent that the leaseholder must pay to the freeholder for the whole duration of the lease. Failure to pay service charges and ground rent on time can result in the forfeiture of the lease, so your solicitor will check carefully that all payments are up to date.

BUYING A PROPERTY IN SCOTLAND

The procedure for buying a property in Scotland is entirely different. Under the Scottish system the seller invites offers and a legally binding contract is created as soon as an offer is accepted. In an active market a closing date is usually set for offers.

On or before the closing date the purchaser's solicitor sends a detailed offer to the vendor's solicitor. This will include the price offered, the date when possession is required and any special conditions (for example subject to survey). There will also be a condition that the vendor's solicitor must provide proof of title and clear searches.

Once the offer has been accepted, letters are exchanged between the solicitors in order to clear up all outstanding matters. These letters are known as 'missives'.

Once both parties are satisfied, the contract is made unconditional – the English equivalent of Exchange of Contracts.

The procedures after contracts have been exchanged are broadly similar to those that apply in England.

The Scottish system is quicker than the English system but it does have several drawbacks. The main ones are:

Wasted costs
Would-be buyers often have to spend quite a lot of money on valuation and survey fees before they can make an offer for a property. If their offer is refused, this money will have been wasted. Many buyers incur abortive survey fees several times before they manage to buy a property.

Co-ordinating the chain
Under the Scottish system it is much harder for buyers to co-ordinate their house purchase with their house sale. The consequence of this is that Scottish buyers have to arrange bridging finance and/or arrange temporary accommodation far more often than their English counterparts.

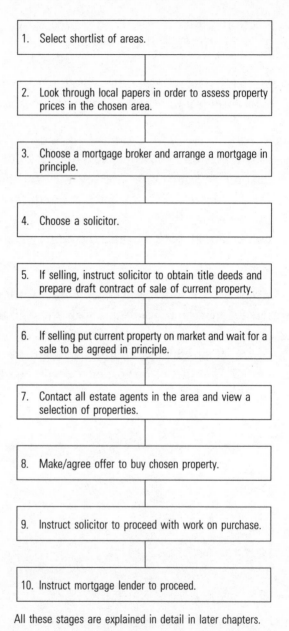

1. Select shortlist of areas.

2. Look through local papers in order to assess property prices in the chosen area.

3. Choose a mortgage broker and arrange a mortgage in principle.

4. Choose a solicitor.

5. If selling, instruct solicitor to obtain title deeds and prepare draft contract of sale of current property.

6. If selling put current property on market and wait for a sale to be agreed in principle.

7. Contact all estate agents in the area and view a selection of properties.

8. Make/agree offer to buy chosen property.

9. Instruct solicitor to proceed with work on purchase.

10. Instruct mortgage lender to proceed.

All these stages are explained in detail in later chapters.

Figure 1. Recommended home-buying process (current system).

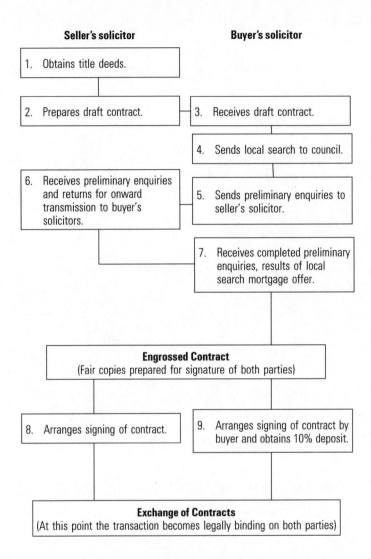

Seller's solicitor   **Buyer's solicitor**

1. Obtains title deeds.

2. Prepares draft contract.

3. Receives draft contract.

4. Sends local search to council.

6. Receives preliminary enquiries and returns for onward transmission to buyer's solicitors.

5. Sends preliminary enquiries to seller's solicitor.

7. Receives completed preliminary enquiries, results of local search mortgage offer.

Engrossed Contract
(Fair copies prepared for signature of both parties)

8. Arranges signing of contract.

9. Arranges signing of contract by buyer and obtains 10% deposit.

Exchange of Contracts
(At this point the transaction becomes legally binding on both parties)

Figure 2. Conveyancing flowchart Part 1.

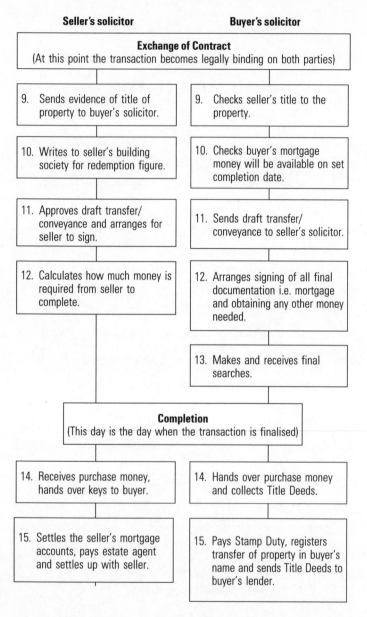

Seller's solicitor	Buyer's solicitor
Exchange of Contract (At this point the transaction becomes legally binding on both parties)	
9. Sends evidence of title of property to buyer's solicitor.	9. Checks seller's title to the property.
10. Writes to seller's building society for redemption figure.	10. Checks buyer's mortgage money will be available on set completion date.
11. Approves draft transfer/conveyance and arranges for seller to sign.	11. Sends draft transfer/conveyance to seller's solicitor.
12. Calculates how much money is required from seller to complete.	12. Arranges signing of all final documentation i.e. mortgage and obtaining any other money needed.
	13. Makes and receives final searches.
Completion (This day is the day when the transaction is finalised)	
14. Receives purchase money, hands over keys to buyer.	14. Hands over purchase money and collects Title Deeds.
15. Settles the seller's mortgage accounts, pays estate agent and settles up with seller.	15. Pays Stamp Duty, registers transfer of property in buyer's name and sends Title Deeds to buyer's lender.

© REATA/NAEA 1996. Used by kind permission of the Residential Estate Agents Training Association and the National Association of Estate Agents.

Figure 2. Conveyancing flowchart Part 2.

$$\left(\begin{array}{c} 3 \end{array}\right)$$

Selling Before You Buy

◆ This chapter deals with selling your current property. If you are buying for the first time go straight to Chapter 4.

◆ If you do have a property to sell, you should read this chapter, then go straight to Part 2 where the procedure for selling a property is explained in detail.

Trying to do things the other way round will almost certainly lead to frustration, disappointment and unnecessary expense.

WHY YOU MUST SELL BEFORE YOU BUY

If you try to buy your next property before you have secured an offer on your current one, you will be disadvantaged at both ends of the transaction.

Many vendors will reject your offer out of hand if you are not in a position to proceed with your purchase immediately. It is extremely frustrating to find your dream home and then be told that you cannot have it.

Even if you do manage to persuade a vendor to accept your offer, your poor buying position might well mean that you have to pay over the odds for the property.

When it comes to selling your current property you will also be at a disadvantage because you will need to sell quickly in order to avoid losing the property that you are trying to buy. This could mean that you are not able to hold out for the best price for the property that you are selling.

The risk of the purchase falling through is also greatly increased. If you are not in a position to proceed immediately, your vendor might well decide to keep the property on the market in case you are not able to sell yours within a reasonable period of time. If someone else in a better buying position makes an offer for the property, there is a high risk that your vendor will choose to accept it. This could leave you with a bill for abortive legal fees and survey fees of several hundred pounds.

Perhaps the worst risk of all though is that your determination to secure the house of your dreams might make you act irrationally.

I have seen countless instances where a buyer has become so determined to secure a property that they have ended up taking out a ruinously expensive bridging loan. There are very few cases where this can be justified.

ACCEPTING A CONDITIONAL OFFER ON YOUR PROPERTY

If you do take my advice to sell first, you need to guard against the risk of not being able to find suitable property to buy within a reasonable period of time. You will also need to guard against the risk of underselling your property.

In a buoyant market there can be periods when property values are rising at the rate of 2% or even 3% per month. If you fix the sale price of your current property then take two or three months to find somewhere to buy, you could find yourself at a considerable disadvantage. In a rapidly rising market it is often best to accept an offer subject to being able to find a suitable property to buy within given period (say four weeks). If you are not able to find a property within the period it may be necessary to renegotiate the sale price agreed with your own buyer.

In a falling market the opposite holds true. If you are not able to find a property quickly your buyer may want to renegotiate the price downwards. However, if you are buying another property yourself you will probably have the compensation of being able to buy your next property at a correspondingly lower price.

The thing to remember throughout is that no one can make you move out of your current property unless you want to. If you really can't find a suitable property to buy, the worst that can happen is that you have to tell your would-be purchasers that you are no longer able to sell them your property.

Whilst you always have this option, it would not be fair to make promises that you know to be false or to cause your would-be purchaser unnecessary cost or inconvenience. The best way to achieve this is to make it clear that acceptance of their offer is subject to being able to find a suitable property to buy. If you have serious doubts about being able to find somewhere suitable, it may also be as well to discourage your purchaser from proceeding with their mortgage application or conveyancing work until you have found somewhere. This will keep both sides' abortive costs to a minimum in the event that the sale does not proceed.

WHAT TO DO IF YOU CAN'T FIND A PROPERTY

If you really can't find a property don't panic and above all else don't buy any old house just to appease your purchaser. A home is far too important a purchase to compromise over and, if you buy the wrong property in a hurry, you might end up having to move again.

If you really can't find a property within the agreed timescale, you will have to decide between one of three options:

Move into temporary accommodation

There is a plentiful supply of high-quality rented accommodation in most areas of the country (see Chapter 1).

Moving twice is inconvenient but your new status as a buyer who can proceed immediately will put you in a very strong negotiating position. Your reward for spending six months in rented accommodation might be the chance to buy a much better property at a much better price.

Negotiate an extension

If you explain the situation truthfully to your buyers, you may be able to persuade them to wait a little longer. For the reasons explained earlier in this chapter, it may be necessary to renegotiate some of the other terms of the sale as well as the timescale.

Withdraw from the sale

The final option is to withdraw from the sale. Your buyers may be angry and disappointed but better this than spending the next 20 years in a house that you don't really like.

IF YOU MUST BUY FIRST

If you really must buy first there is a high probability that you will end up facing the choice between losing the property that you are trying to buy or taking out a bridging loan.

My advice would nearly always be to let your dream house go. As the old saying goes 'houses are like buses, another one will always come along eventually'.

If you are determined to proceed with your purchase you will probably need to arrange a bridging loan. There are two different types of bridging loan, a 'closed loan' and an 'open loan'. A closed loan is a loan that is made for a set period of time. This type of loan is designed for the situation where you have exchanged contracts on both your purchase and your sale but need money to complete on your purchase before you receive the proceeds from your sale. This type of loan is relatively low risk for the lender and closed bridging loans are reasonably easy to obtain.

The best place to obtain such a loan is often your current or new mortgage lender or your own bank. Despite the relatively low risk, closed bridging loan finance is still expensive. Another drawback is that the interest must be paid on a monthly basis – it is not usually possible to add it to your mortgage.

If you have not even exchanged contracts on your sale, you will need an open bridging loan, i.e. a loan for an unspecified period of time. This type of loan is much riskier for the lender. You might never be able to sell your current property and go bankrupt under the strain of paying two loans. Because of this, open bridging loans are much harder to obtain and much more expensive. There are a number of specialist lenders operating in this market but the best place to start may again be your current mortgage lender or your bank.

It is to be hoped that in the future lenders will develop specialised bridging loans that are both more affordable and easier to obtain. The ideal would be to allow the cost of a closed bridging loan to be added to the mortgage on the next property and repaid over the entire period of the next loan.

Case study

Sue and Steven O wanted to move from a three-bedroom semi to a four-bedroom detached house in Guildford, Surrey. They were aware that they ought to sell their current property first but decided to go and view a few properties just to see what they could get for their money next time. The very first house that they saw was absolutely perfect. It had everything they had ever wanted in a house and a fabulous landscaped garden looking out over open fields. They were convinced that they would never find another house quite like it.

Much against their better judgement they put an offer in for 5% less than the asking price. The vendor rejected it out of hand and said that if they wanted her to wait until they had sold their own property she would require the full asking price.

Steve and Sue were determined to have the property so they agreed to offer the full asking price. They immediately put their own property up for sale at £10,000 less than the estate agent's recommended figure in order to try and achieve a quick sale. They also applied for a mortgage on the new property and instructed solicitors to start work.

Three weeks later they received a call to say their vendor had received an offer from someone who was in a position to proceed immediately and that she had decided to take it. They had still not received an offer on their current property and try as they might Steve and Sue could not persuade their vendor to wait any longer.

Commenting on her experience six months later, Sue said 'I wish we had never seen the original property. Apart from the stress and frustration we ended up with a bill for abortive legal fees and survey fees of more than £400 and probably sold our current property for less than it was worth [it's very difficult to increase an asking price]. The final irony though is that the house we did eventually buy is much nicer than the one we lost. Next time we will be sure to sell first'.

Case study

Robin C bought a delightful house in Chelsea in the summer of 2002. He had not sold his current flat but it was in a very popular area and he felt confident that it would sell quickly. Furthermore the house that he was buying was for sale at such an attractive price that he felt able to justify the cost of a bridging loan.

What Robin had not bargained for was the weakening of the London property market which occurred in the second half of 2002. His flat remained unsold for six months and the cost of the open bridging loan was crippling. Eventually he sold his flat in January 2003 for 15% less than the original asking price.

Commenting on his experience Robin said 'With hindsight buying the house before I sold the flat was a bad decision. Although the house seemed a bargain the cost of the bridging loan has swallowed up all my paper profit and has left me so short of funds that I have not even been able to furnish the new house properly'.

$$\boxed{4}$$

Financing the Purchase

Your mortgage will probably be the biggest financial commitment that you will ever make. This chapter will show you how to choose the right loan from the thousands of options that are available. Getting your loan sorted out before you start looking seriously will put you in a better position to buy and save a lot of time later on.

ARE YOU CREDITWORTHY?

If you are deemed to be 'uncreditworthy' your choice of mortgage lender will be severely restricted. Indeed it may not be possible to borrow money at all. Mortgage lenders will determine whether you are creditworthy in one of three ways.

Credit scoring

Credit scoring is the process by which a mortgage lender looks back at all its previous cases and tries to identify the factors that make people statistically more likely to default on their loans. It then designs a process which awards applicants black marks for each matching feature in their personal circumstances.

For example the lender's research might show that people who are self-employed are statistically twice as likely to default on their loans as people who are employed. Accordingly applicants who are self-employed will be given 20 black marks on their credit score.

Further research might show that people who are less than 25 years of age are statistically three times more likely to default on their loans as people who are older. Accordingly applicants who are less than 25 years will be given 30 black marks on their credit score.

Each mortgage lender has its own credit scoring process and each awards 'black marks' for different criteria. However, generally speaking you will lose points if:

+ You are self-employed.
+ You have changed jobs recently.
+ You have an unstable employment record (i.e. you have changed jobs frequently)
+ You have moved home recently or often.
+ You are not on the electoral register.
+ You have never had a mortgage or any other loan.
+ You are single or cohabiting with a partner.

You will be given black marks each time your personal circumstances match one of the above criteria. If your total credit score falls below a certain level, the lender will decline your mortgage application.

Credit scoring is a crude and sometimes unfair process. From time to time stories appear in the press about Sir Rupert Whoever, Chairman of Megabucks plc who earns a million pounds a year but was refused a small mortgage because he has just changed his job and moved house.

Despite these occasional glitches, credit scoring is a cheap and, statistically speaking, fairly accurate way to assess how likely an applicant is to default on their mortgage payments and it seems likely that most mortgage lenders will continue to use it.

A good mortgage broker should be able to warn you if your personal circumstances make you likely to fail a credit scoring test and advise on what action to take in order to avoid your application being rejected.

Financial references

In addition to 'credit scoring' your application, the mortgage lender will also take up financial references. These will include

◆ A search to make sure that you have never been declared bankrupt.

◆ A search to make sure that you do not have any County Court Judgements for debt (CCJs).

◆ A search to make sure that payments due on any previous loans have been made on time.

This information is available to lenders 'on line' from any of the country's credit reference agencies.

By far the greatest number of problems with financial references occur because of County Court Judgements for debt. Many thousands of people have County Court Judgements for debt registered against them that they are completely unaware of. The root cause of the problem is the ease with which a County Court Judgement for debt can be obtained.

If you have a County Court Judgement for debt registered against you, your choice of mortgage lender will be severely restricted. If you have just one County Court Judgement for debt, if you disclose it on the mortgage application, if the sum involved is relatively small (usually less than about £2,000) and if the debt has been 'satisfied' (i.e. repaid in full) then it may still be possible to obtain a loan with a mainstream mortgage lender.

If you have more than one County Court Judgement against you, if the sum involved is more than about £2,000, if the debt is still partly or wholly outstanding or if you did not disclose the CCJ on the mortgage application form (even if you did not know of its existence) your mortgage application will normally be refused.

In such cases your only option will be to apply to a mortgage lender who specialises in 'credit impaired' cases. The interest rate charged on such a loan will almost certainly be much higher than that charged by the mainstream lenders and such a mortgage should be considered only as a last resort.

Employment references
The final check that the mortgage lender will make is to take up references from your employer. In order to avoid problems and delays you need to ensure that your employer responds to the reference request immediately and that they complete the lender's official form rather than just sending the information in letter form.

HOW MUCH CAN YOU BORROW?

For many years most mortgage lenders lent a maximum of three times your income plus once the income of your spouse. On this basis a couple earning £20,000 and £10,000 respectively would be able to borrow £20,000 × 3 = £60,000 plus £10,000 × 1 = £10,000 i.e. a total of £70,000. These limits may seem over cautious. They are not. They are sensible limits designed to prevent borrowers from over stretching themselves.

A young couple who are both in secure employment may feel confident enough to borrow far more than this. However, they have no way of knowing what the future may bring.

♦ Interest rates might rise causing their mortgage payments to increase enormously.

♦ An unplanned pregnancy might require one partner to give up work sooner than they had planned.

♦ Redundancy or illness could reduce the family's income without warning.

Some mortgage lenders will now lend as much as four times the first income and one times the second. On this basis the couple earning £20,000 plus £10,000 could borrow a maximum of £90,000 (£20,000 × 4 plus £10,000 × 1).

Some mortgage lenders will lend as much as 3 times joint income. If you and your spouse both earn similar salaries this method of calculation will enable you to obtain the largest possible loan. For example if both partners earn £20,000, the maximum loan obtainable would be £120,000 (£20,000 plus £20,000 equals £40,000 × 3 = £120,000).

The risk of mortgaging yourself up to the hilt might be justified if:

◆ You have good reason to believe that your income will rise rapidly in the future.

◆ You are confident about the security of your employment.

◆ You have insurance to protect your income in the event of redundancy or illness.

◆ You have protected against the risk of rising interest rates by taking out a fixed rate mortgage (see page 47).

In all other cases it may be safer to stick to the borrowing limits imposed by the mainstream mortgage lenders.

Treatment of overtime and commission payments

A great deal of confusion is caused by the way that mortgage lenders treat overtime and commission payments. If your employer states that overtime or commission is 'guaranteed' most lenders will treat it as if it were basic salary. If it is not 'guaranteed', most mortgage lenders will only allow half its value when calculating how much you can afford to borrow.

For example:
Miss A earns £10,000 basic salary plus £10,000 guaranteed commission, so she can borrow 3 × £10,000 plus 3 × £10,000, i.e. £60,000.

Miss B earns £10,000 basic salary and £10,000 non-guaranteed commission, so she can borrow $3 \times £10,000$ plus $1\frac{1}{2} \times £10,000$ i.e. £45,000.

If any part of your salary is paid by way of overtime or commission you need to check with your employer on whether this will be described as guaranteed or non-guaranteed before you apply for a mortgage.

Self-employed applicants
Most of the mainstream lenders require self-employed applicants to provide three years audited accounts to confirm their income. If you cannot do so your choice of mortgage lender will be restricted.

If you have recently become self-employed, or if you cannot prove your income you really need to speak to a specialist mortgage broker in order to determine what options are available. Many self-employed applicants end up taking a 'non-status' mortgage. This means that the mortgage lender relies on the value of the property for their security rather than on the income of the applicant. Non-status loans are normally limited to a maximum of 75% of the value of the property (i.e. you will need to be able to find the deposit of at least £25,000 to buy a £100,000 property).

Maximum loans as a percentage of the property's value
Few mortgage lenders will lend more than 95% of the property's value. This means you will have find a deposit of £5,000 in order to purchase a £100,000 property. Some lenders will lend 100% of the purchase price but because

they perceive 100% mortgage as being higher risk, the cost of borrowing will usually be higher.

The opposite is also true. If you need to borrow less than about 75% of the value of the property that you are buying you may be able to get a lower interest rate which reflects the lower risk to the lender.

Some lenders will lend more than 100% of the purchase price of the property. However, such loans are normally restricted to people who are in negative equity (i.e. they own a property which is worth less than the mortgage outstanding on it). If you are in such a position you need to seek the advice of a specialist mortgage broker regarding the options that are open to you.

Indemnity guarantee premiums

If you need to borrow more than a certain percentage of the purchase price, you may need to pay a mortgage indemnity guarantee premium. The 'trigger point' varies from lender to lender but is usually around 75%–80%.

Indemnity insurance protects the building society *but not you* against the risk of losing money if you default on your mortgage and the property is resold for less than the mortgage outstanding.

Indemnity guarantee premium rates vary considerably from lender to lender so it pays to shop around. Some will allow the premium to be added to the loan. Some insist that it is paid in cash. Some lenders have stopped charging for indemnity insurance altogether although the cost may be recouped elsewhere in the loan.

THE ROLE OF THE MORTGAGE BROKER

Approximately 40% of all mortgages are still arranged direct with a mortgage lender rather than through a mortgage broker. I find this astonishing.

If you walk into a bank or building society and say 'I'd like a mortgage please' you will only be told about the mortgage products that are available through that bank or building society. If you walk into the ABC Building Society they are certainly not going to say 'The XYZ Building Society are offering a much better rate that we are at the moment, why don't you go and talk to them?'.

Approximately 150 mortgage providers compete for customers in the UK mortgage market. Most of these 150 providers offer a variety of different types of mortgage schemes (see page 46) and this means that there are at least 1,500 different mortgage options to choose from. The chance of finding the mortgage that is best for you by walking into a bank or building society at random is at least 150 to one against.

Before you choose a mortgage, I would urge you to speak to a mortgage broker. A good mortgage broker will look across the whole mortgage market and advise on which mortgage is best for you.

Where to find a mortgage broker

Most mortgage brokers fall into one of four categories:

♦ Independent mortgage brokers – look in the *Yellow Pages* under Mortgage Brokers.

- Independent financial advisers – look in the *Yellow Pages* under Financial Advisers. Before making an appointment, check that the firm specialises in the mortgage market.

- Solicitors – some solicitors have a Financial Services Division. Check that the person that you will be seeing specialises in the mortgage market before you make an appointment.

- Estate agents – most estate agents have an in-house mortgage broker. Note: it is not necessary to buy a house from an estate agent in order to use their mortgage broker. Most will be delighted to arrange a mortgage for you even if you are buying a house from one their competitors.

HOW TO CHOOSE A MORTGAGE BROKER

Choosing the right mortgage broker could save you many thousands of pounds over the full mortgage term and a great deal of time and frustration in the shorter term. It is therefore well worth taking some care over your choice. Here are some questions that you can ask that will help you to make the right choice:

- Are you able to advise me on the mortgage products that are available from all the 150 UK mortgage lenders? If not how many mortgage lenders do you have access to?

- Do you have access to 'mortgage sourcing software' i.e. a computer programme that will give up-to-date advice on the latest schemes that are available and help you to assess which one is the best for me?

- How many different lenders did you deal with last year (the answer should be at least a dozen)?

- What percentage of all your mortgage lending do you refer to the top four lenders? (Note: some brokers place most of their lending with just three or four lenders and in return received an enhanced level of commission – known as a procuration fee.)

- How long have you been a financial adviser?

- Approximately how many mortgages did you (and/or your firm) arrange last year? (Note: some financial advisers specialise in other areas such as pensions and arrange very few mortgages. Such advisers are unlikely to have the experience necessary to advise you on the best mortgage scheme.)

- What professional qualifications do you have?

- Are you an independent financial adviser or an appointed representative of just one life assurance company? (Note: in an ideal world you would want to deal with an independent financial adviser who specialises in the mortgage market. However, such firms are few and far between. If you have to compromise, it is usually better to choose a broker who specialises in the mortgage market and is an appointed representative of a well-known insurance company rather than an independent financial adviser who knows little about the mortgage market.)

- How will you charge me for your work? (Note: most brokers will be paid a commission for selling you an insurance policy. They often also receive a smaller commission from the mortgage lender. Some brokers also charge an arrangement fee. This is particularly common when the commission that can be earned is small. Some brokers, particularly IFAs, have a policy of refunding all commissions to the client and charging for their advice on an hourly basis. They believe that this helps to ensure impartiality.)

◆ Why should I arrange my mortgage through you?

Before you make a final decision you should try to see two or three brokers and ask these questions to each of them. The time to do this is when you first start looking for a property. Do not wait until you have found somewhere. Choosing a mortgage is a decision that is too important to make under pressure.

The vast majority of mortgage brokers will be happy to spend half an hour with you describing their service without charge and without obligation. Those that are not are not worth dealing with.

HOW TO CHOOSE A LENDING SOURCE

Before making a recommendation a good broker will consider many different criteria including:

Type of lending scheme required

The two most common options are variable rate and fixed rate. The interest rate charged on a variable rate mortgage will fluctuate in line with the base rate set by the Bank of England. In September 2003 the cost of a variable rate mortgage was around 5.5%. However, mortgage rates in the past have been as high as 18%. Interest rates could rise to this level again. Just imagine the consequences if they were to do so. Someone currently making mortgage payments of £550 per month would have to pay £1,800 per month. Where would they find another £1,250 per month from? The consequence could be the loss of their home.

The main alternative is a fixed rate mortgage. As the name implies, the interest rate is fixed for an agreed period. This could be anywhere from 1–25 years. If interest rates rise during this period, you would be the winner. If they fall, you would end up paying more than you needed to for your mortgage. For example:

Mr A fixes at 7% for one year and makes payments of £7,000 per annum or £583.33 per month.
Interest rates rise immediately to 10%.
Payments would have been £10,000 per annum or £833.33 per month.
Mr A however continues to pay £583.33.

By the end of the year he has saved 3% i.e. £3,000.[2]

A lot of people try to out-guess the markets. This is not the right reason to take out a fixed rate loan. A fixed rate loan gives you the security that your mortgage payments will not rise for a given period. If interest rates fall, the saving that you could have made becomes the price that you paid for that security. If interest rates rise during the period of the fix you have got a bonus.

---

2. This is a simplified example. Due to the way that interest rates are calculated the real interest payments would be a little different to this.

The question to ask yourself therefore is what period, if any, do I need the security of a fixed rate mortgage for.

◆ You may want to fix for the whole mortgage term.

◆ You may want to fix for just the first three to five years, i.e. the period when the burden of paying a new mortgage will be heaviest.

◆ If you can comfortably afford the repayments, you may not want to fix at all.

A good mortgage broker will advise you on whether to take a fixed or variable rate mortgage and what period to fix for. If you decide on say, a five-year fix, he will then compile a list of mortgage providers who offer competitive rates for a five-year fixed term.

Constraints imposed by each lender's lending criteria

Each of the mortgage lenders have their own quirks about the type of property that they will lend on. These are based mostly on any bad experiences that they have had with loans that have gone wrong in the past.

Examples of the type of property that some mortgage lenders will not lend on would include:

◆ Property built before 1919.
◆ Property that is above commercial premises.
◆ Any property with a thatched roof.
◆ Any property worth more than a certain value.
◆ Any property outside a certain geographical area.

Your mortgage broker will check that the property that you are buying meets the lending criteria of your proposed lender. If you are buying an unusual property you may find that your choice of mortgage lender is severely restricted.

Constraints imposed by your personal or financial circumstances

As I explained earlier in this chapter your choice of mortgage lender will be severely restricted if you are self-employed, if you have any County Court Judgements for debt or if you want to borrow more than three times your salary.

Current interest rate

Having compiled a shortlist of possible lenders, the broker should go on to compare the interest rate that is currently being charged by each. Interest rates vary hugely between different mortgage lenders. The additional cost over the term of the loan can be enormous. For example on a £50,000 mortgage a 1% increase in the interest rate paid would mean extra payments of:

- £42 per month
- £500 per year
- £12,500 over the full term of the loan.

In September 2003, the current interest rates charged by different mortgage lenders varied by nearly 5%. This would mean extra payments over 25 years of £62,500 on a £50,000 loan! This example is an extreme one but shows how important it is to shop around.

Historic interest rates

It is important to remember that a mortgage is a 25-year commitment. It would be a grave mistake to choose a mortgage lender who is offering a cheap interest rate now but puts it up as soon as you have taken out your loan. A good mortgage broker will be able to advise you on which mortgage lenders have offered consistently competitive mortgage rates.

Discounts/cash/free insurance/waiver of fees

The mortgage market is fiercely competitive and many mortgage lenders try to attract new borrowers by offering various discounts and other incentives. Most of these take one of four forms.

Discounts

The lender may offer a discount of say 5% for the first year. This means that instead of paying say 8% you pay only 3%. This can be tremendously useful if you have spent all your money on new furniture, carpets and curtains.

Cashbacks

Another way of giving a discount is a cashback. This means that on completion you will receive an agreed sum back in cash. This is another way to fund the cost of furnishing and redecorating a new property.

Free insurances

A third way of giving a discount is through free insurances. For example the lender may say that it will pay the premiums for buildings insurance for the first say five years.

Waiver of fees
The fourth way of giving a discount is for the lender to waive the cost of the survey fee and/or the arrangement fee.

Some lenders offer a package of incentives that includes a combination of all of the above.

Clearly, trying to calculate whether a 5% discount for the first year is worth more than no survey fee and free buildings insurance for the next five years is extremely difficult. In fact, the calculations are so complex that even the mortgage broker will probably use a computer program in order to determine which package offers the best value.

Special conditions
The next criteria that the broker will consider is whether the proposed mortgage lender has imposed any special conditions on the loan. These often onerous conditions are sometimes buried in the small print. Two of the most common are.

Redemption penalties
If you repay the mortgage within the first (say) five years, you might be liable to pay a redemption penalty. This can be one, three, six, nine or even twelve months' interest. Your broker's job is to draw your attention to all such conditions. If you are planning to move again within the redemption period your broker may advise you to chose a different mortgage lender.

Compulsory insurances
The second common trick is to insist that you take the

lender's buildings or contents insurance for the whole of the mortgage term. The cost of the policy is often far more than the cost of a similar policy elsewhere. If this is the case, your broker may advise you to consider an alternative mortgage lender.

Efficiency of services

The average time taken to process a mortgage application varies hugely between different mortgage lenders and even between different branches of the same mortgage lender. The most efficient regularly process applications in less than ten working days. The least efficient often take six to eight weeks.

Every extra day that you are waiting for a mortgage offer is an extra day when something can go wrong. It is therefore essential to choose a mortgage lender with a reputation for efficiency. Your broker will be able to advise you on which lenders meet this criteria.

Aftersales service

Some mortgage lenders have a reputation for poor aftersales services and inefficient administration. An example of such inefficiency would be a lender which 'forgets' to collect the mortgage payments by direct debit for several months and then takes all the payments in one go. Dealing with the consequences of such maladministration can be very stressful and time-consuming. Your broker should be able to steer you away from lenders with a particularly poor reputation for aftersales service.

Summary

At the time of writing there are more than 2,000

alternative mortgage options and at least eight different criteria to consider – a total of at least 16,000 pieces of information to consider. From this it should be clear that an informed choice can only be made after speaking to a professional.

CHOOSING A REPAYMENT METHOD

Once you have decided on a lending source, you need to decide on how you are going to repay the money. For most people the decision will be between one of three options:

Repayment mortgage

A repayment mortgage is the simplest type of mortgage. Your borrow say £50,000 and each year pay back interest on the loan and a little bit of the capital that you borrowed in the first place. Consider this simplified example:

Example 1

A £50,000 loan is made over a term of 25 years

This means that on average each year the capital repayment is £50,000 ÷ 25 years, i.e. £2,000 per annum On top of this interest is payable at 10%

Thus in the first year the payment is £5,000 interest
£2,000 capital
repayment
──────
£7,000 total

The problem is that a repayment mortgage does not work like this. In order to keep the mortgage payments down in the first years, the mortgage lender reduces the amount of capital that is repaid in the early years of the loan. As the loan decreases, the amount of interest payable each year decreases, and a larger percentage of the repayment becomes available to repay the capital.

Example 2

The same £50,000 loan is made over a 25-year term. The interest rate is still 10%

The first year's payment is   £5,000 interest

                                            £500 repayment

                                                  of capital

                                   £5,500 total

Whilst this certainly makes the mortgage payments more acceptable, the drawback is that if the borrower moves house again two or three years later they might find that they have repaid very little of the £50,000 that they originally borrowed.

On moving, they would probably take out a new 25-year loan and the whole process would start all over again. If they move house on a regular basis they might still be paying off a mortgage at an age when they wish to retire.

A repayment mortgage might be the best choice if you intend to stay in the same property for some time. However, before you make a final decision you should consider the alternatives of an investment backed mortgage or a pension linked mortgage.

Investment mortgages

With an investment mortgage, the same £50,000 is borrowed over the same 25-year term. However, the full

£50,000 loan remains outstanding for the full 25 years. The average £2,000 per annum that would have been used to repay the capital is instead invested in an investment policy (usually either an endowment policy or an ISA). This money is used to buy stocks and shares (and in certain cases other investments such as property). The hope is that in 25 years' time the value of the investment policy will have increased to a level where it can be used to repay the £50,000 mortgage and possibly provide a surplus for the policy holder to spend as he wishes.

Investment mortgages have two main benefits. The first is that they give the policy holder a chance of receiving a cash sum over and above the sum necessary to repay their mortgage at the end of the term. The second advantage is that with an investment mortgage, the repayment date is fixed no matter how many times you move house again in the future. If you do move again, you simply carry on paying the premiums and take out a new mortgage for the sum required to purchase your next home. Any additional mortgage money required can be borrowed on either a repayment basis or an investment basis and repaid over whatever term is convenient. For example:

Mr B takes out £50,000 investment mortgage at the age of 25. The term is 25 years and his mortgage will be paid off when he is 50. Five years later he decides to buy a larger property with a £100,000 mortgage. The original investment policy will pay out £50,000 when he is 50 years old, i.e. in 20 years' time. The other £50,000 could be funded by:

- Another £50,000 investment policy over 25 years. He would be able to pay £50,000 back when he was 50 years old and the other £50,000 when he was 55 years old.

- Another £50,000 endowment over 20 years. This would mean that he would able to repay the whole £100,000 at the age of 50.

- A £50,000 repayment mortgage repayable over whatever term was convenient.

Endowment policies have in the past been an excellent investment for some policy holders. Consider this (true) example. An endowment policy was taken in January 1974 with a top performing insurance company. The sum assured was £50,000 and the term was 25 years. The policy matured in January 1999. The policy holder received just over £160,000. This gave him £50,000 to repay his mortgage and £110,000 to spend as he pleased.

Unfortunately stock market returns have been considerably lower in recent years than they were during the 1970s and 80s. In the last three years world stock markets have fallen significantly. As a consequence many people, who took out endowment policies during the last ten years have found that their policy will not even provide enough money to repay their mortgage, never mind providing any surplus. These policy holders are faced with the choice between increasing the level of premiums paid into their policy or paying off the shortfall from their own resources. As a result investment backed mortgages have fallen out of favour in recent years and currently make up only a small percentage of total mortgage lending.

No one knows how the stock markets will perform over the next 25 years. An investment mortgage may or may not be right for you but before you take such an important decision you need to take advice from a suitably qualified professional.

Pension mortgages
The last option is a pension mortgage. The main advantage of a pension mortgage is that it is very tax efficient. Under current legislation you will receive tax relief on your pension premiums at your highest marginal tax rate.

There are at least three disadvantages. These are:

Future eligibility
Pension mortgages can only be funded from a personal pension policy. These are usually taken out by the self-employed or by those whose employer does not provide a company pension scheme. If at some future time you decided to become a member of a company pension scheme, you would have to cease making payments into your personal pension plan and make alternative arrangements to repay your mortgage.

Affordability
A pension mortgage will cost more than an endowment mortgage or a repayment mortgage. The reason for this is that under current legislation only one third of a pension fund can be taken on retirement as a cash lump sum. The remainder must be used to purchase an annuity (this may change in the future). The mortgage can only be repaid from the cash lump sum. Thus, in order to fund a pension

mortgage of £100,000, one would need to build a pension fund of £300,000.

Income in retirement
Many people feel that the whole of their pension should be used to fund their retirement. By using one third of your pension fund to repay a mortgage you will significantly reduce your income when you retire.

Investment return
If you do decide to take out an endowment mortgage or a pension mortgage, it is extremely important to choose a provider with good investment performance. More than 100 life assurance companies compete to offer endowment and pension products in the UK market and their performance varies greatly.

Three factors will determine the return that your policy achieves.

Risk to reward ratio
Some policies are low risk and low reward. The most conservative policies are usually the traditional with profits policies. These policies reduce risk by investing in property as well as in the stock market. Risk is reduced further by the fact that once a bonus has been allocated to your policy it cannot be taken back again.

'Unit linked' policies are higher risk but are projected to earn a higher return. These policies usually invest entirely in the stock market. Furthermore, the whole of the fund is reinvested each year (rather like an accumulator bet). This means the previous gains could be lost.

The highest risk policies are those that invest in areas such as small companies or emerging markets. In a good year performance can be spectacular but in a bad year losses can be huge or even total. Because of the risks very few home buyers choose this type of policy.

There is a very close correlation between the risk that you are prepared to take and the reward that you receive.

Investment performance
By picking the right shares an insurance company can achieve way above average performance in any sector. The investment performance of different life companies varies enormously. Some companies are consistently better performers than others but, unfortunately, there is no such thing as the best company over all.

Most companies have a wide range of different funds and an insurance company that has a reputation for good performance might still have some poorly performing individual funds. There is also a balance to be struck between star performance and consistency. A fund that is consistently in the top ten is likely to achieve better performance than a fund that is top one year and bottom the next. Tables are available that rank every company and every fund by performance. Your financial adviser will help you to interpret them.

Charges
Insurance companies make a charge for managing your money. These charges are very hard to compare and vary hugely from one company to another. The benefit of outstanding investment performance can be negated

entirely by high charges. Your financial adviser will be able to help you to avoid the highest charging companies.

Summary
The decision regarding which repayment method is best for you is a complex one and it is essential to take advice from a suitably qualified professional before making a final decision.

MORTGAGES IN THE FUTURE
I would predict that there will be two significant changes in the mortgage market in the future.

The first is that mortgage lenders will be forced to design more flexible loans. The days when one could expect a job for life have long gone and today's working arrangements are far more varied and flexible. Many people are not employed but work on a contract basis. Many people have more than one job. An increasing number of people are becoming self-employed. These changes will require the development of flexible mortgage products that allow borrowers to make higher mortgage payments when they are able to do so and stop making payments entirely when they are between jobs. This is already starting to happen.

My second prediction is that the government's attempt to speed up the home-buying process will put pressure on lenders to get mortgage offers out more quickly. In practice this is likely to mean that most buyers will choose a mortgage lender and allow that lender to take employment and financial references before they start looking for a property.

Case study

Carl B bought a brand new three-bedroom detached property for £75,000. On the advice of his father Carl arranged a mortgage through the ABC Building Society without shopping around. Two months later whilst chatting to his new neighbour Carl discovered that he was paying £60 per month more for his mortgage than he need have done.

Commenting on his experience Carl said 'I had no idea that mortgage rates varied so much. Next time I will shop around more carefully.'

Case study

John McD bought a two-bedroom flat for £30,000 in 1996. He had a County Court Judgement for debt for £1,200 incurred as a result of a dispute over a second-hand car which broke down. He had paid off the debt 18 months ago but knew that his CCJ would affect his mortgage application.

John arranged his mortgage through a small mortgage broker out of the local paper. In view of his CCJ John was thankful to be offered any loan and didn't flinch at the interest rate which was 3% above the norm.

Three years later John met his future wife and they decided to buy a house together. This time they went to a much larger mortgage broker and again John declared his CCJ. 'That will no problem at all' said the broker. 'In fact, if you'd come to me three years ago, I could have arranged a loan for you through a major lender. I don't know why you took out the loan that you did'.

John was furious. During the last three years he had paid £2,700 more than necessary for his mortgage. There is no doubt that next time he will see more than one broker.

(5)

Deciding What to Buy

This chapter will help you make the right compromise between the property that you want and the property that you need.

WHAT SORT OF PROPERTY DO YOU REALLY NEED?

We all have a dream home – a penthouse flat, an old rectory, or perhaps a farmhouse set in its own land. But whilst it is nice to dream, unless you have just won the lottery, this is not the property that you will actually buy. For most of us buying a property means making a series of trade-offs and compromises.

The best way to decide on what compromises you are and are not prepared to make is to set your requirements down on paper. See Figure 4 for how the list might look for a family with two young children looking to buy a three or four bedroom suburban house. (Try doing this exercise yourself using the same headings.)

THE IMPORTANCE OF LOCATION

The three most important factors in valuing a property are location, location and location. So says the old estate agents' adage and this one is 100% correct.

A smaller property in a better area will nearly always be a better buy than a larger property in a poorer one. There are at least four good reasons for this.

Need	Want
BEDROOMS	
Minimum 3. The children (a boy aged six and a girl aged four) are sharing a bedroom now and cannot do so for much longer.	4. A guest room would be nice but frankly guests do not come to stay with us all that often. A sofa bed in one of the living rooms would probably suffice.
LIVING ROOMS	
2. The only living room in our current property is always strewn with toys and it is driving us mad.	3. In addition to a playroom a separate dining room that could also be used as a study would be wonderful. Frankly though it would not be used all that often.
KITCHEN	
Must be large enough to eat in unless there is a separate dining room.	The bigger the better.
BATHROOMS	
1	With two young children a ground floor toilet would be really useful and a second bathroom even better.
GARAGE	
Not essential	A garage would be nice but it would mostly be used for storage so a garden shed would do.
GARDEN	
60 ft minimum – the same as we have now.	The bigger the better.
TYPE OF PROPERTY	
1930s semi because it strikes a good balance between spacious rooms and reasonable maintenance costs.	Would love a detached property but its probably out of the price range.
CONDITION	
Reasonable order throughout. We are not DIY enthusiasts and getting the builders in is too expensive. Would redecorate but not much more.	Something that is in spotless condition throughout.
LOCATION	
Must be in the catchment area for All Saints Primary School and the James Brown Secondary School.	Would really like to live on the Avenue Gardens estate if we can afford it.
SITUATION	
We have a dog, a cat, and two young children. We would not be prepared to live on a main road.	A cul-de-sac would be ideal.
TRANSPORT LINKS	
We would like to be close to the station.	We only use the station two or three days each month so its proximity is not essential.

Figure 4. List of requirements.

Social benefits

Most people are happiest living in an area where there are other people like them. For example, if you have a young family it's nice to know that there are other young families in the area. It would be much harder to feel at home in an inner city area where the majority of your neighbours are students.

Fear of crime

Crime or more accurately the fear of crime is another important factor which is encouraging people to head for the relative safety of the established residential areas.

Schooling

Until recently we were lead to believe that all schools were the same. The publication of the school league tables has dispelled this myth forever and property within the catchment area of the better schools is increasing in value disproportionately.

Investment

For reasons that I shall explain later in this chapter, the value of property in better residential areas has been increasing more quickly than the value of property elsewhere. This trend looks set to continue. A smaller property in a better area is therefore likely to be a better investment.

The choice of location will of course involve an element of compromise. A one-bedroom flat in Mayfair might be an excellent investment but it would hardly be an appropriate place to bring up a family. Nevertheless, when it comes to choosing the location the fewer compromises that you can make the better.

Spotting the up-and-coming areas

The desirability of an area can change very quickly. I can think of a suburb of Manchester where property has halved in value during the last five years. The problem started when a housing association bought a few houses and moved some problem tenants in. The existing residents found their new neighbours difficult to live with and those that could sold their properties and left the area.

The sudden increase in the number of properties available led to a drop in prices and this in turn made the area more attractive to the housing associations who bought up more properties. This changed the residential mix of the area permanently and the last of the original residents felt so uncomfortable that they also left. Today the area is almost entirely owned by housing associations and is controlled by problem tenants. It is now such an undesirable place to live that values have plummeted.

The opposite can also occur with equal speed. A good example of an area where prices increased very rapidly would be West Acton in west London. West Acton is next to Ealing which has always been a desirable area. Most of the houses are large Victorian and Edwardian properties with four or five bedrooms.

During the 1970s and 80s many of the houses were considered too large for single family occupation and were split up into flats and bedsits. Now the trend is being reversed. Prices in Ealing had risen to such a level that many families could no longer afford to buy there. West

Acton was a logical alternative. The properties were very similar to those in Ealing. Transport links were good and the area was within the catchment areas of some good schools.

The trickle of professional families moving into the area became a flood and prices increased sharply. The original residents, mostly young people living in small flats, no longer felt at home and began to move out to more cosmopolitan areas. Today West Acton is almost indistinguishable from Ealing.

If you are young, single or married without children and want to gamble on buying a property in an up-and-coming area, you need to look for an area that is adjacent to a good area, has good transport links and has access to good schools. If you already have a family, my advice would be to stick to established residential areas.

HOW TO ASSESS AN AREA

If you don't know the area that you are intending to buy in, it is well worth spending some time getting to know it properly. First impressions can be very deceptive and ideally you should visit the area at least three times, once on a weekday, once at night and once at a weekend.

It is surprising how many apparently quiet streets are plagued by problems such as commuter traffic during the rush hour or gangs of marauding teenagers after dark.

Here are some other useful ways to size up an area.

- Visit the local shops – do they sell the sort of things that you buy?

- Visit the local pubs – do you feel at home with the locals?

- Look at the gardens – are they well maintained and what play equipment is there? This will give you an idea of the ages of the local children.

- Count the number of bells on each door – more than one means that the house has been split into flats. This could mean noise and parking problems.

- Look (discreetly) through the windows – the curtains, decor and furnishings will give you a good idea of the age and background of the people who live there.

- Check out the local transport – try actually doing the journey to work before you commit yourself.

- Check out the schools – the league tables are not perfect but they give a good idea of the quality of schooling in the area.

FACTORS THAT MAY REDUCE THE ASKING PRICE

Location is not the same as situation. By comprising over the situation, you might well be able to avoid making compromises in other areas. For example a house on a busy road might sell for 20 or 30% less than an identical house around the corner. Places to look for bargains include:

- on a busy road
- near a railway line
- under a flight path

- out of easy reach of shops
- outside the catchment area of good schools
- next to an industrial or business site
- above a shop.

YOUR HOME AS AN INVESTMENT

Your home is probably the most expensive thing that you will ever buy and you will naturally be anxious to ensure that it turns out to be a good investment. Some research that I did for a *Sunday Times* article confirms the importance of choosing a property in the right location.

We looked at a number of properties bought 15 or 20 years ago and compared their value then to their value today. The results were fascinating. One of the most dramatic results was obtained in Bristol. At one end of the scale we found an example of a two-bedroom flat in Redland, a prosperous suburb, bought for £8,500 in 1979 and by 1999 worth £80,000, an increase of 941%.

At the other end of the scale, we found a three-bedroom house in Southmead, a less desirable area nearby, valued at £18,000 in 1982 and sold at £18,500 in 1997. An increase of just 3% over 15 years.

The conclusion of this research was clear. Property in the best residential areas has appreciated in value much more quickly than property elsewhere. On this basis I say again; whatever you compromise on do not comprise over location, location or location.

Case study

Marilyn and Philip B had intended to buy a three-bedroom house in Chiswick but they fell in love with a six-bedroom house in a less desirable area close by. The house had previously been used as bedsits and required a lot of work but it had potential and they felt that such a beautiful house would always be easy to resell.

They began to feel unwelcome in the area almost as soon as they moved in. Most of the properties were still arranged as bedsits. They had nothing in common with their neighbours and there were no other children for their girls to play with. The local school was awful. The walk to the station took 15 minutes. A week after they moved in Philip's car was vandalised. The final straw came five months later when they were burgled in broad daylight.

Marilyn and Philip decided to cut their losses and move again. The property proved extremely difficult to sell. It took four months to find a buyer and they did not recover the money that they had spent on refurbishment.

Commenting on her experiences Marilyn said 'It was such a beautiful house but we just could not put up with the area. We have lost money on the house and had to pay two lots of moving costs. It has been a financial disaster. We are now buying the house in

Chiswick that we should have bought in the first place. As a result of our mistake we have a much larger mortgage than we need have had.'

Case study

Simon and Katrina J were determined not to compromise over the area. They bought a three-bedroom semi-detached house in Wilmslow, a very desirable and expensive part of Cheshire. The house was smaller than they would have liked but they felt that location was all.

The area was lovely but the house drove them mad. Their two youngest children had to share a bedroom and fought like cat and dog half the night. The dining room became a playroom and the kitchen was not large enough to eat in. The result was that they had to eat most of their meals off their laps. The worst thing though was that Katrina, a freelance journalist, had no proper place to work. She had to put a desk in the corner of her bedroom but she found it hard to work in the room that she slept in and hard to sleep in the room that she worked in.

After 12 miserable months Simon and Katrina decided to move again, this time to a four-bedroom, three-living room Victorian house in a pleasant but cheaper town, ten miles away.

Commenting on her experience Katrina said 'we took the adage of location, location and location too much to heart and ended up with a house that was too small for our needs. I am cross that we have had the expense and inconvenience of moving twice but there is no doubt in my mind that moving again was the right thing to do'.

(6)

Finding a Property

Once you have decided what type of property you are looking for this chapter will help you to find it.

GETTING THE BEST OUT OF ESTATE AGENTS

As I explained in Chapter 2, estate agents are not on your side. The estate agent's job is to get the best price for the vendor. Nevertheless, in order to achieve this, estate agents need to be nice to purchasers so that they will view the maximum number of properties. There is strong correlation between the number of viewings that are arranged on the property and the price that is achieved.

For your part you need to make friends with all the estate agents. By doing so, you will help to ensure that you are told about all the new properties that come up for sale. The more properties you see, the better will be the chance that you will choose the right one.

How estate agents assess their purchasers

Even in a quiet market, estate agents are contacted by far more purchasers than they can service effectively. Most therefore operate a grading system to separate the wheat from the chaff. A typical grading system would work like this:

Grade 1 – Hot

Definition: Purchaser is able to proceed with a purchase immediately. This means that you:

♦ are a first time buyer
♦ have sold your own property and have a completed chain
♦ are in rented accommodation
♦ are able to proceed without selling your current property.

If you fit into this category you should be told about every new property as soon as it comes onto the market.

Grade 2 – Local vendors

Definition: Local vendors cannot proceed immediately because they have their own property yet to sell. If you are a local vendor it means that you:

♦ have a house to sell locally which is not yet on the market.
♦ have your house already up for sale with another estate agent.
♦ have your house already up for sale with the same agent that you are trying to buy through.

If you fit into this category you should receive good service from the agents that you contact. However, you should be aware that the agent's prime objective may be to persuade you to instruct them to sell your current property. You are not a hot buyer until you have secured an offer on your own house.

Grade 3 – others

Definition: This category covers all purchasers who are moving from out of the area and have a house yet to sell.

If you are not yet in a position to buy and have no property to sell that the agent can earn a fee on, you will not be a priority for most agents. Some agents will refuse point blank to register you as a buyer until you have got an offer on your own property. Others will register you, but refuse to arrange any viewings until you have sold. This can be extremely frustrating. However, you must see it from the estate agent's point of view. The agent knows that statistically 95% of people who register from out of the area will never buy a property in his town. The only way to ensure that you are taken seriously is to secure an offer on your own property before you start looking seriously.

The registration process

It is best to register with the estate agents in person if possible. You will be able to strike up a much better rapport face to face and this will help to ensure that you are the first person that the agent thinks of when a new property comes onto the market. By registering in person you may also get to see details of properties that have only just come onto the market and are not yet ready to be circulated.

The agent will ask you a number of questions and will (discreetly) grade you as a 'hot buyer', 'potential vendor' or 'other'. If you are a hot buyer or a potential vendor you may be offered the opportunity to view some properties immediately. It is well worth doing so if you have the time. By agreeing to view immediately, you will help to consolidate the agent's impression that you are a serious buyer. Your feedback will also give the agent a more accurate idea about precisely what type of property you are looking for.

Do try to make sure that you register with all the agents in the town, even if they don't appear to specialise in the sort of property that you are looking for. The most up-market agents occasionally deal with bread-and-butter properties and vice versa. Often such an agent will have relatively few applicants for these properties and this could mean that you pick up a bargain.

Agent's particulars
Once you have registered, the agent should send you particulars of all the new properties that come onto the market in your price range. It is likely that you will receive particulars of many properties that do not meet even your most basic requirements (a two-bedroom flat when you wanted a four-bedroom house). There is no point complaining to the estate agents about this. Many agents deliberately avoid selecting which properties to send in case you are tempted by a long shot.

Since the Property Misdescriptions Act was introduced agent's particulars must by law be accurate. Misdescription of a property is a criminal offence and agents' details can these days be relied upon.

Telephone contact

Even in a quiet market the best properties come and go very quickly, sometimes before the details have even been prepared. It is therefore essential to ensure that you leave telephone numbers where you can be contacted at any time of day. If you are really anxious to move, it may even be worth telephoning all the agents periodically to see if anything new has come in. As the old saying goes, the creaky wheel gets the grease. A telephone call once or twice a week will certainly confirm that you are a serious buyer and will help to ensure that you are in the front of the estate agent's mind when a new property does come onto the market.

Urgency

The best properties really do sell very quickly, sometimes within hours. If you are offered a chance to view somewhere, it is therefore worth trying to fit in a viewing as soon as possible, even if this means viewing after dark. If the property seems a possibility, you can always return in daylight.

How to behave during a viewing

You would be well advised to say as little as possible when you are viewing a property. If you express enthusiasm for the property, the agent and/or the vendor might take a tougher stance during subsequent negotiations because they believe that you want the property badly.

If on the other you complain loudly about the poky rooms and tired decor, the vendor may be offended and decide that they do not want to sell the property to you at all. All in all the best thing is keep your thoughts to yourself.

Feedback

A good agent will call you after every viewing to get your feedback. If the agent doesn't ring you, ring him. When giving feedback try to cover the things that you did like as well as those that you didn't, but be honest. Unless you give honest feedback, the agents will not have the information that they need in order to find you the right property.

BUYING PRIVATELY

The great majority of properties are sold through estate agents, but it is certainly possible to buy a property privately. Private sellers are not always aware of the true value of their property and bargains can occasionally be had.

There are three ways to go about finding a property privately.

◆ **Private advertisements** – most local papers have a privates sellers section at the back.

◆ **Advertise yourself** – it might be worth trying your own 'wanted' advertisement in the local paper. Describe the property that you are seeking, state your price range and make it clear that you are a private buyer and that no commission will be payable.

◆ **Leaflet drop** – the most successful way to find a property is to leaflet drop houses in the road that you are interested in. Again, remember to make it clear that you are a private buyer and that no commission will be payable.

USING THE INTERNET

Many house buyers now start their property search on the Internet. There is no doubt that the Internet is becoming more important with each month that goes by but at the moment hunting for a property on it can be a frustrating experience.

The majority of estate agents have their own Internet site which allows house buyers to view the properties that the agent has available. In addition most agents subscribe to one of the major property portals. There are four major portals but most properties are advertised on only one of them. In order to find all the properties available in an area the Internet buyer will probably have to look on a dozen or more different sites. The problem is compounded by the fact that a lot of sites are badly out of date and display properties that have been sold several weeks previously. The only sure way to find out about all the properties that are for sale in an area is to telephone the estate agents directly.

RETAINING AN AGENT TO ACT FOR YOU

If you do not have the time, the market knowledge or the inclination to look for a property yourself, you could retain an agent to do the job for you. Retained agents, or property search agents as they are often known, tend to specialise in the upper end of the market. If you are looking for this type of property, a good search agent can earn their fee many times over. They will:

◆ Advise you on which areas to consider.
◆ Advise you on schools, transport and other amenities.

- Help to agree a realistic budget.
- Compile a shortlist of properties.
- Often obtain details of properties not on the open market.
- Conduct the first viewing on your behalf.
- Advise on what price to pay.
- Negotiate the purchase on your behalf.
- Help to ensure that the sale goes through smoothly.

The fee for this service will typically be 1½ to 2% of the purchase price plus VAT. Most search agents require a non-refundable deposit before they start work.

COMPILING A SHORTLIST

Once you have viewed a good selection of properties (preferably at least half a dozen) you should be ready to compile a shortlist. Often the decision is made on the basis of a gut reaction. Some American research found that 50% of all house buyers had made a decision to buy before they got inside the front door and 75% had made a decision before they left the first room. However if you are having difficulty deciding between more than one property, it may be useful to compare each against your original criteria (see Chapter 5).

One very important last factor to consider is the owners. Do you trust them? How well does their timescale match yours? If you need to be in within four weeks and their new home will not be ready for three months, you may need to find somewhere else.

Case study

Julie and Patrick M were in a tearing hurry to buy a property. They had moved to Bath from London and were renting a flat from Patrick's employer. They very much wanted a home of their own. They registered with every agent in the area in person and Julie telephoned them all twice a week. Their persistence paid off when a delightful three-bedroom cottage came onto the market. The agent telephoned Julie at 9.30 a.m., both she and Patrick viewed at 1.30 p.m. and made an offer at 2.30 p.m. The offer was accepted the following morning and they moved in six weeks later.

Commenting on her home-buying experience Julie said 'I probably made a bit of a nuisance of myself but it paid off in the end. We are delighted with our new home'.

Negotiating the Purchase Price

This chapter will help you to make sure that you pay a fair price for your chosen property.

HOW TO ASSESS THE VALUE OF A PROPERTY

Comparables method
Estate agents value properties by comparing them against similar properties in the area. These properties fall into two categories: properties that are currently for sale in the same price range and are therefore competing for the same buyers and properties that have recently been sold where the actual price achieved is known. You need to make your assessment of the value of the property that you are intending to buy using the same method.

Before you make your offer try to obtain as many details of other properties in the area as possible. Ask the estate agents to give you particulars of houses that have recently sold or look on the Land Registry site, *www.landreg.gov.uk*, where actual selling prices can now be obtained. How do the various properties compare? If you are buying an estate type property you may be able to find comparables that are almost identical to the one that you are considering. Valuing this type of property is relatively easy.

Adjustment factors
If you are intending to buy a more individual property, you will need to apply a number of adjustment factors to the comparable properties that are available. Some of the most important factors to take into account are listed below:

Extensions and improvements
The full cost of extensions and improvements will not generally be recovered. The proportion of the original cost that is recovered will depend upon the nature of the improvement. For example:

High cost recovery (up to 100%)
◆ Addition of extra bedroom in a style that is in keeping with the original property.
◆ Addition of central heating.
◆ Redecoration in a neutral style.
◆ Addition of a garage.

Medium cost recovery (up to 50%)
◆ Addition of ground-floor flat-roofed extension.
◆ Addition of conservatory.
◆ Fitted kitchen.
◆ Modernisation of bathroom.
◆ Loft conversion.

Low cost recovery (less than 25%)
◆ Addition of outdoor swimming pool.
◆ Addition of ground floor bathroom.
◆ Double glazing.
◆ Cavity wall insulation.

Some improvements can substantially reduce the value of the property, for example:

♦ Extensions that occupy the entire garden.
♦ Stone cladding.
♦ Double glazing on period property.
♦ Removal of period features (fireplaces, decorative plasterwork, etc.)

Repairs
As with improvements, the full costs of repairs made to the property is unlikely to be recovered. Many buyers underestimate the cost of repairs and some are prepared to pay a premium for a house in poor condition in order to have the satisfaction of refurbishing it to their own taste.

Area
In many towns a house in one road can command a very substantial premium over houses in the next. It is impossible to generalise about this but the boundaries are usually well-known locally.

Location
A house on a busy road or one backing onto a railway line will be worth substantially less than an identical house in a quiet street nearby. An extremely adverse location could reduce the value of a property by up to half.

New developments
Many people will pay a premium to live in a brand new house. All new developments must therefore be excluded from your comparable evidence.

Square footage/meterage method

A method of valuation that is used extensively abroad but quite seldom in the UK is square footage. If you are having difficulty coming up with a value for an unusual property, it may be worth calculating the price per square foot. Divide the asking price by the total floor area. For example:

Asking price	£100,000
Floor area	1000 square feet
Price per square feet	£100

Then try doing the same calculation for similar properties that are for sale in the same price range.

Ask the vendor

One final option is to ask the vendor or the estate agent to justify the price that is being asked. Say that you are thinking of making an offer and the price looks a little steep and ask them how they arrived at their figure. What supporting evidence are they able to provide? Do their arguments seem convincing?

MAKING AN OFFER

It is best to make the initial offer in writing if possible, This will help to ensure that your offer is communicated accurately and will help to avoid future misunderstandings or disputes about who said what. In the interests of speed a fax is best.

The initial letter should:

♦ Be clearly marked 'subject to contract'.

- Summarise the benefits of your buying position and your timescale.
- State the price offered.
- Justify the price offered.
- List any other conditions.

For example:

Dear Mr Jones,

Re: 27 Avenue Gardens, Anytown
SUBJECT TO CONTRACT

I should like to make an offer to purchase your property.

I am in an excellent position to proceed quickly. I am in rented accommodation at the moment and I have no property to sell. I have a large deposit and my mortgage is already arranged. I could probably exchange contracts within four to six weeks.

I should like to make an offer of £65,000. I feel that this is a fair price for the property because a sale was agreed at this figure on 17 Avenue Gardens three weeks ago. Number 34 is also up for sale at £65,950.

My offer is subject to survey and subject to you taking the property off the market immediately.

I hope that my offer is acceptable to you and I look forward to hearing from you shortly.

Yours sincerely,

P Smith

Figure 5. Letter making an offer to purchase.

It is usually best to make all offers via the agent who has a statutory obligation to pass them on.

HANDLING THE NEGOTIATIONS

The traditional process of negotiation is highly confrontational. The parties start off a few thousand pounds apart and each side takes turns to increase or decrease the price that they are prepared to pay or accept.

The problem is that each concession makes the parties more determined not to give in again and all too often the negotiations reach deadlock. Sometimes the issue left unresolved is trivial to the point of farce. Most estate agents can tell a story about a sale that did not proceed because of a dispute over a garden shed, a tired old stair carpet or even a wooden toilet seat.

The way to avoid this is to keep asking the simple questions 'why' and 'how'. If the vendor rejects your first offer, ask them why they have rejected it and how they have arrived at the figure they require. The correspondence might continue like this:

Dear Mr Smith,

Re: 27 Avenue Gardens, Anytown
SUBJECT TO CONTRACT

Thank you for your offer to buy our property. I am afraid that we cannot afford to take less than £69,000.

Yours sincerely,

Mr Jones

Figure 6. Letter refusing an offer.

Dear Mr Jones,

Re: 27 Avenue Gardens, Anytown
SUBJECT TO CONTRACT

I am sorry to hear that you cannot accept our offer. Before I consider increasing it, could you tell me how you arrived at your valuation of £69,000.

I look forward to hearing from you,

Yours sincerely,

P Smith

Dear Mr Smith

Re: 27 Avenue Gardens, Anytown
SUBJECT TO CONTRACT

17 Avenue Gardens was in poor condition and required redecoration. No. 34 has no garage. I feel therefore that our property is worth £69,000.

Yours sincerely,

Mr Jones.

Dear Mr Jones,

Re: 27 Avenue Gardens, Anytown
SUBJECT TO CONTRACT

I agree that No. 17 was in poor condition and on this basis I am prepared to raise my offer to £67,000. I feel that this is a fair offer and I hope that you will now accept it. May I remind you again that we can move very quickly.

Yours sincerely,

P Smith

Figure 7. Series of letters negotiating an offer increase.

Dear Mr Smith,

Re: 27 Avenue Gardens, Anytown
SUBJECT TO CONTRACT

Thank you for your revised offer which I am prepared to accept provided that
you exchange contracts within six weeks. Please contact my estate agent to
arrange all the final details.

Yours sincerely,

Mr Jones

Figure 8. Letter accepting an offer.

The technique of asking the other party to justify their
position works like a magic charm and can be used
several times during the same negotiation.

HOW TO COMPETE WITH OTHER WOULD-BE PURCHASERS

Even in a quiet market, the vendors of the best properties
often receive more than one offer. The way to get your
offer accepted is to sell the benefits of your buying
position to the vendor. For example, if you know that the
vendor needs to move quickly, stress the speed with which
you can move.

By finding out what the vendor is hoping to achieve and
making your buying position match these needs, you will
often be able to get your offer accepted without increasing
the price.

Sealed bids

When a property is in great demand, the agent will
sometimes advise going to sealed bids. Would-be purcha-

sers are asked to make their best and final offer in writing by a given date. The difficulty when deciding what offer to make, is that you do not know what other parties have offered. If you are determined to secure the property a good way to do so is to bid an odd amount, e.g. £111,111. Most people bid in round figures so you might win the contest by a £1.

When making a sealed bid remember to include details of your buying position. The vendor is not obliged to accept the highest bid and if you are in a strong position he may decide to accept your offer even if he has a higher one.

WHEN TO WALK AWAY

It is all too easy to get caught up in a bidding fever. A client of mine once sold a house on the River Thames at Henley for more than twice its asking price because two people were absolutely determined to have it. You may be able to justify paying a little over the odds to secure a house that you love but there comes a point when it is better to wait for the next one to come along.

Another thing to bear in mind is that if you agree to pay significantly over the odds, the property could be down-valued by the building society surveyor and this may prevent you from proceeding with the purchase anyway.

Case study
Sharon W viewed a flat that was on the market at £49,950. During the viewing the vendor made the

mistake of telling Sharon that they had just had an offer accepted on a house that they really loved.

Knowing that the vendor was in a hurry to move Sharon decided to try a cheeky offer of £40,000. The vendor rejected it out of hand and said that the offer was so insulting that he would not now consider selling Sharon the flat at any price. Three days later the flat was sold to someone else for £48,000.

Commenting on her experience Sharon said 'I liked the flat and it was worth £49,950. With hindsight I wish that I had gone in with a more reasonable opening offer'.

Case study

Sanjay P made an offer to pay £110,000 for a house that was on the market for £130,000. He had researched the offer carefully and felt that his offer was a fair one. The vendor rejected it out of hand and said that he wanted the asking price.

Sanjay asked the vendor to justify his figure of £130,000. The vendor said that this was the price that he needed in order to buy his next property. Sanjay pointed out that this was no reason for him to pay over the odds and cited two comparable properties that had sold recently for £110,000 and £112,000 respectively. The vendor would not budge and Sanjay walked away.

Three weeks later Sanjay had an offer accepted to buy a virtually identical property in the next street at £112,500. The property that he walked away from remains unsold.

(8)

Choosing a Solicitor

A good solicitor will make your purchase quicker, less stressful and much less likely to fall through. This chapter will help you to make the right choice.

THE IMPORTANCE OF CHOOSING THE RIGHT SOLICITOR

There are two key dangers that you need to guard against. The first is a solicitor who is slow, inefficient, or unnecessarily pedantic. A consequence of instructing such a solicitor could be that you lose the property that you were trying to buy.

An even worse danger is posed by the solicitor who is overworked, inexperienced in conveyancing matters or does not check the documentation carefully enough. If you instruct a solicitor like this, you could end up buying a property that later proves to be impossible to resell.

HOW TO CHOOSE A SOLICITOR

Choose a specialist

If you had a brain tumour you would seek the advice of a brain surgeon. You would not expect your family doctor to perform the operation on you himself and you would certainly not seek advice from an osteopath just because he happened to be a family friend.

For exactly the same reasons if you were buying a property you should not automatically go to your local family solicitor and you should almost certainly avoid using the solicitor who you met whilst he was advising your employer on their taxation affairs. Conveyancing is a specialist area of the law and you need a conveyancing specialist not a general practitioner or a tax specialist.

Before you instruct a solicitor to handle your conveyancing work, check to make sure that the firm specialises in residential conveyancing. This means that it has at least one person in the firm who deals with conveyancing 100% of the time. Such firms will have come across all the common problems before and will have the systems and knowledge necessary to have the best chance of resolving any problems that may come up with your purchase.

Ask for recommendations

One of the best ways to choose a solicitor is by recommendation. If you know someone who has bought a house recently, ask which solicitor they used and what they thought of them. It is also well worth asking your estate agent and/or mortgage broker for a recommendation. They deal with solicitors on a daily basis and will have a very good idea of which local firms are most efficient.

Never choose on price alone

Fees for conveyancing work vary enormously but a conveyancing solicitor should never be chosen on price alone. If a solicitor gives a quote that is significantly cheaper than his competitors it will usually mean one of two things:

- Most of the work will be handled by an unqualified (and therefore cheaper) legal assistant.

- The solicitor has budgeted to spend less time on your case.

The consequences of this could be:

- Documents might be examined less thoroughly.

- It might be hard to get hold of your solicitor if you have any questions or if a problem needs to be resolved.

- The sale might take longer than necessary to go through.

- The chances of making a mistake are increased.

The adage you get what you pay for holds true in most areas of life and it certainly holds true when choosing a conveyancing solicitor.

Get more than one quote
These days most solicitors are very pleased to give you a quote over the telephone. Try to ring at least three firms if possible. The brief conversation that you have with each will help to ensure that you pick someone who you feel comfortable with as well as comparing fees.

Choose early
It is best to choose a solicitor before you start looking seriously for a property. If you are selling a property as well as buying, your solicitor will be able to start work on obtaining the title deeds and preparing a draft contract.

This will save time once you find a buyer.

Even if you are buying for the first time, it is best to find a solicitor before you find somewhere. Choosing a solicitor is such an important decision that it is best to avoid having to do it in a hurry.

Questions to ask before instructing a solicitor

Ask to speak to a partner in the conveyancing department. Say that you are buying a property and want a quote for conveyancing. The solicitor will probably start by asking you some questions about the property so that he can give you an accurate quote.

Here are some questions to ask once he has finished:

◆ What does the quote include?

◆ What does the quote exclude?

◆ Does the firm specialise in residential conveyancing?

◆ Roughly how many conveyancing cases does the firm deal with in a typical year?

◆ Ask if the firm is on the 'panel' for the mortgage lender which you are intending to use (if they are not the mortgage lender will probably want to instruct another solicitor to protect their interest, which will cause unnecessary delay and add to the cost).

◆ Who will actually handle the work?

◆ Why should I instruct your firm to handle my conveyancing rather than the other firms that I have spoken to?

THE ALTERNATIVES TO INSTRUCTING A SOLICITOR

The great majority of house buyers (about 90%) currently use a local conveyancing solicitor. However, the conveyancing market is changing quite quickly and there are now a number of alternatives. These include:

Licensed conveyancers

The Society of Licensed Conveyancers was set up to break the solicitor's monopoly of the conveyancing market. In practice they have captured only a small share of the conveyancing market. Most licensed conveyancers work for small local firms and offer a service that is quite similar to that offered by solicitors. Like solicitors many compete on price rather than on service.

Solicitors' marketing agencies

The first solicitors' marketing agency was set up in 1993. Several now operate in the UK market. The marketing agency obtains conveyancing work both by approaching estate agents and by advertising its service direct to the public. The actual conveyancing work is passed onto independent firms of conveyancing solicitors who are appointed on a panel basis. The solicitors' marketing agency charges a mark up on the cost of the solicitor's work. In return, they employ a customer care team whose job it is to keep the customer informed of all progress on their sale or purchase.

The main benefit of dealing with a solicitors' marketing agency is that they are open very long hours and offer high levels of customer service. The drawback is the additional cost.

Estate agent-owned conveyancing operations

Countrywide Assured, the UK's largest firm of estate agents, set up its own conveyancing division in 1997. Countrywide took the solicitors' marketing agency concept one stage further by employing its own team of licensed conveyancers rather than passing out the work to outside firms. It seems likely that other estate agency firms will soon start to offer a similar service.

This type of operation offers several important benefits including convenience, long opening hours and generally high standards of customer care. They can also speed up average transaction times. Countrywide has agreed detailed protocols (e.g. semi-standardised pre-contract enquiries) with three independent firms of solicitors. In cases where one party is using Countrywide and the other party is using one of these three recommended firms, average transaction times have been reduced quite considerably. The main drawback again is cost.

National conveyancing firms

At the time of writing two major firms of solicitors (Eversheds and EDC Lord) have just opened their own express conveyancing operations to compete with the type of operation set up by Hambros. Both will offer long opening hours, enhanced service levels and a dedicated customer care team to keep clients informed of all progress. Despite the premium fee levels I would predict that this type of operation, which competes on service rather than price alone, will quickly take a significant share of the conveyancing market.

Doing your own conveyancing

It is perfectly possible to do your own conveyancing. Provided that you are buying a freehold property with registered title, the procedures are quite straightforward and DIY conveyancing guides are available to help ensure that you complete all the necessary stages correctly.

However, in practice, very few people handle their own conveyancing. There are three reasons for this. The first is that where a mortgage is involved, the mortgage lender will insist on employing a solicitor to protect its interests. You will be expected to pay for this. This reduces the potential saving on legal fees considerably.

The second reason is that the consequences of missing something can be appalling. At worst you could end up buying a property that proves to be impossible to resell.

The third problem is that other people involved in the transaction may take a dim view of you handling your own conveyancing. The estate agent may advise the vendor not to accept your offer for fear that your inexperience of conveyancing matters might delay the sale. The solicitor acting for the other side might also be deliberately pedantic in order to try to trip you up.

Taking everything into account there are very few circumstances where I would advise you to handle your own conveyancing.

Case study

Colin A bought his first home in 1988. The property was a two-bedroom first floor flat which had been newly converted from a Victorian two-storey house. Colin rang round for conveyancing quotes and took the cheapest one. The solicitor that he chose was not terribly helpful. It was extremely hard to get hold of him and when he did answer the phone he sounded harassed and eager to end the call. On several occasions he failed to return Colin's calls. Nevertheless the purchase eventually went through.

Four years later Colin's employers offered him a better job in Newcastle. Colin decided to sell the property. A sale was agreed very quickly. This time Colin used a different solicitor.

Two weeks into the sale Colin received a phone call from his estate agent. The agent said that the buyer had pulled out due to a defect in the lease.

Colin rang his solicitor for an explanation. To his horror he learned that the lease should have given him the right to walk across the front garden, which was owned by the ground floor flat in order to reach his front door. Unfortunately the developer who sold him the flat had forgotten to put this clause in the lease and his original solicitor had failed to notice. According to the terms of the lease Colin had no right to use his own front path in order to reach his own front door.

Before he could sell the flat, Colin had to apply to his freeholder for a 'Deed of Variation', i.e. permission to change the defective clause in the lease. His freeholder demanded payment of £1,000 for his 'inconvenience' plus legal costs. The total cost was nearly £1,500. On top of this Colin's sale was delayed by six months. As a result his employer withdrew the job offer in Newcastle.

Commenting on his experience Colin said 'My original solicitor was clearly negligent. As a result I have been left £1,500 out of pocket and my promotion at work has been delayed. I shall be pursuing a claim for damages against my original solicitor, but God only knows how long it will take or whether I will eventually be successful. I have learnt the hard way about the importance of choosing a solicitor with care'.

9

Choosing a Surveyor

This chapter will help you to decide what type of survey you need and give advice on how to choose the right surveyor.

DO YOU REALLY NEED A SURVEYOR?

If you are buying a property for cash, you could buy without a survey. However, you would be most unwise to do so. The vast majority of cash buyers do instruct a surveyor to check the property over before they exchange contracts.

The confusion sets in when a mortgage is involved. If you are buying a property on a mortgage, the lender will insist that a surveyor visits the property to undertake a valuation for mortgage purposes. Many people assume that this is all the protection that they need – in fact approximately 80% of all home buyers do not instruct their own surveyor and rely entirely upon the building society's report and valuation. They are wrong to do so.

The purpose of a building society report and valuation is to confirm to the mortgage lender that the property that you are buying is satisfactory security for the mortgage advance that is to be secured upon it. Thus if you were buying a property for £100,000 and applying for a £30,000 mortgage, the surveyor's job is to confirm that the property is worth at least £30,000. Well of course it is. If the house fell down tomorrow the site would be worth £30,000.

Before you buy the property you need to know rather more than this. Specifically you need to know:

◆ Is the property worth the price that you are paying for it?

◆ Are there any serious structural defects that might affect your decision to proceed with the purchase?

◆ Are there any less serious defects and if so approximately how much will they cost to rectify.

The only way to establish this information will be to instruct your own surveyor.

WHAT TYPE OF SURVEY DO YOU NEED?

Home buyer's report
The RICS/ISVA Home Buyer's Report is prepared in a standard format in order to keep costs down. The main objective of the home buyer's report is to:

◆ Reassure you that you are paying a fair price for the property.

◆ Inform you about any serious defects that may affect your decision to proceed with the purchase.

◆ Inform you about any less serious defects which may affect the price that you are prepared to pay for the property.

A home buyer's report is likely to be the most appropriate choice if the property that you are buying is:

- built after 1919
- of a traditional construction
- free from obvious structural defects.

In 2003 the typical cost of a home buyer's report for an average sized property was around £300 plus VAT. In addition to buying peace of mind, many buyers find that they are able to recoup the cost of their survey by using it as a negotiating tool in subsequent price negotiations.

Building survey

A building survey is more comprehensive than a home buyer's report and is not prepared in a standard format. A building survey may be the best choice if:

- The property you are buying was built before 1919.

- The property is of a non-standard construction (e.g. it has a thatched roof or stone walls).

- The property is in poor condition and/or has an obvious structural defect (e.g. a crack in the wall or a wonky door or window frame).

- The property is particularly large or expensive.

The typical cost of a building survey on an average sized property in 2003 was £400 plus VAT. The cost of a building survey on a very large or unusual property could be several times as much.

Structural engineer's report

If the surveyor suspects that the property may have a structural defect he may advise you to commission a specialist structural engineer's report. A structural engineer will assess whether the defect presents a risk to the future stability of the building and advise on what action needs to be taken in order to rectify the problem.

From a safety point of view surveyors and structural engineers tend to err heavily on the side of caution. There is no doubt that much of the repair work that they advise is unnecessary.

However, from a resale point of view any property with a structural defect may prove extremely difficult to sell and unless the property that you are considering is exceptionally good value you should think very carefully before proceeding.

The cost of a structural engineer's report will vary considerably according to the nature of the fault that they are investigating. Ask for a quote before you proceed.

Quantity surveyor's report

If the property that you are buying requires very extensive works, it may be worth instructing a quantity surveyor to prepare a detailed 'Bill of Works'. This is a detailed estimate of the likely costs. A Bill of Works may help you to renegotiate the purchase price. It will also help you later on when it comes to getting building estimates and supervising the work.

Timber report

It is quite common for a surveyor to ask for a timber report.

If there is evidence of woodworm, wet rot or dry rot a specialist company will be called in to assess the extent of the problem and the cost of rectifying it.

The thing to bear in mind here is that most timber companies provide reports free of charge and are paid only if they are employed to deal with the problem. It is therefore in their interest to find work that needs doing. The problems that they are likely to find fall into three categories.

Woodworm

Many older houses have had an attack of woodworm at some time in the past. Woodworm is easy to spot. The affected wood has lots of tiny holes almost as if somebody has been throwing darts at it. It can affect any internal or external timber, for example floorboards, windows, doors etc. Unless the owner is able to provide a written guarantee that the problem has been treated it is highly probable that you will have to treat the wood again. Fortunately woodworm is relatively cheap to treat.

Wet rot

Wet rot is caused by the prolonged exposure of untreated timber to rainwater or severe damp. It can affect any external timber or internal timber that has become exceptionally damp. Timber that has not been regularly painted is particularly susceptible.

Wet rot is fairly easy to spot, the timber feels damp and spongy to the touch. It may be treated either by a local builder or by a specialist timber treatment company.

Dry rot

Dry rot is caused by a fungus called Serpula Lacrynens. It is by far the most serious of the three problems and the most expensive one to treat. Dry rot is caused when a damp void such as a cellar, the space beneath the floorboards or a chimney breast is left without sufficient ventilation.

Dry rot is easy to recognise. Affected timbers have distinctive cracks which go along and across the grain causing tiny oblong shapes. The fungus itself looks like a flat white pancake. There is also often a heavy musty smell. The problem is that the attack often starts beneath a floor or inside a chimney breast and as not discovered until it has caused extensive damage.

Treatment involves replacement of all the affected timber. In order to ensure that the attack does not reoccur it is also necessary to strip off the plaster and pull up floors in adjacent areas so that the timber can be treated with a chemical preventative. If anything is missed, the dry rot will reoccur.

The cost of treating a dry rot can run into many thousands of pounds. If the property that you are buying has dry rot the safest thing to do is to run a mile. If you do not, be sure to get detailed estimates before proceeding.

Damp reports

It is also common for the surveyor to ask for a damp report. If the moisture content of the walls seems unusually high, the surveyor will recommend that a specialist damp company should be called in to identify the cause of the problem and estimate for the cost of rectifying it.

Like timber companies, most damp companies undertake surveys free of charge and are paid only if they find work that needs doing. This means that they have a vested interest in finding work that needs to be done. The problems that you are most likely to find come into three categories:

Rising damp

Rising damp is caused when the damp course breaks down and the bricks in the walls, which are porous, start to suck up water from the ground. In time, the dampness rises to a level approximately one metre above the ground.

Severe cases are easy to spot. Wallpaper becomes discoloured and starts to peel off the walls. Paint becomes discoloured and often starts to blister. Some home owners try to disguise the problem by putting on lots of layers of wallpaper or even panelling the lower half of the walls. Treatment involves injecting a chemical into the base of the wall to stop the dampness and replacing the plaster up to a height of about one metre.

The problem is that this treatment is often recommended when moisture levels are much lower. In such cases the best thing to do is often to just live with the problem. A second problem is that the cause of dampness might be something altogether different (see below) and the treatment proposed quite unnecessary.

The best advice is:

◆ Check for other sources of dampness before proceeding.

◆ If the problem is not serious try living with it for a bit before acting.

◆ Get more than one estimate before proceeding.

Penetrative damp
This type of dampness is caused by a leaking roof, gutter, window frame or something similar. It will normally be rectified by a local builder rather than by a damp company. The treatment is to find and rectify the cause of the leak then to replace the affected plaster.

Damp caused by incorrect ground levels
A very common cause of dampness is incorrect ground levels. If the level of the ground outside is above the level of the damp course, dampness will be sucked up from the ground. Before proceeding with any damp treatment go outside and look for the damp course. In most buildings this will run horizontally around the building about six inches or so above the ground. Look for a line of bitumen or slate between two courses of bricks. If the ground level is higher than the damp course in any area it will need to be reduced.

BUYING A BRAND NEW PROPERTY

The great majority of new properties are protected by an NHBC warranty. If the property that you are considering does not have a NHBC certificate, you should proceed only with the greatest of caution. It will be essential to commission your own survey in order to check that the property has been built to a satisfactory standard. Even if the survey does give the property a clean bill of health, you need to bear in mind that a new property which does not have an NHBC certificate might be quite difficult to resell.

If the property that you are buying does have an NHBC warranty it will be guaranteed for ten years against structural defects and there is therefore probably no need to commission your own structural survey.

However, it is important to appreciate that the NHBC warranty only covers major defects. It does not cover the cost of rectifying the more minor teething problems that seem to affect so many new homes.

There are five things you can do to reduce the chance of buying a defective new home:

◆ Buy from a developer with a reputation for quality. The new homes industry runs its own awards scheme.

◆ Don't just view the show home. Ask to inspect several other properties on the site before you buy and make your own assessment of the quality of the finish.

- Try to talk to other people on the site and ask if they have experienced any teething problems with their properties. If so, how efficiently did the developer deal with them?

- Telephone the aftersales office on some pretext or visit it if it is on site. These are the people who will be responsible for rectifying any defects. Their attitude speaks volumes about the developer's attitude to customer service.

- Consider visiting other developments built by the same developer in the area. Do they still look bright and new? Again try to talk to some of the residents and see if they have had any problems.

CHOOSING A SURVEYOR

Surveyors are not all the same and it is well worth taking some time to find a good one. Ask your solicitor, your mortgage lender, your estate agents and any friends who have brought a property recently for recommendations and make sure that you ring several firms before you make a final decision. Here are some questions that you can ask:

- Are you on the panel for the mortgage lender that I am using? This is very important. If the surveyor is on the panel (i.e. approved by your mortgage lender) he will be able to carry out the home buyer's report or building survey at the same time as he undertakes the mortgage valuation. This will save both time and money.

- Where are you based? A local surveyor will know about any specific problems that affect the local housing stock. He is also likely to have a better idea of local values than someone who is based many miles away.

◆ How quickly could you get me the report? Every day's delay is another day when something could go wrong.

◆ Can I telephone you to discuss the report? This is also very important. If any aspect of the report is unclear, you must be able to clarify it.

◆ Why should I instruct your firm to carry out my survey? A good answer would include issues such as experience, local knowledge and quick turn around times.

◆ How much will it cost? Fees vary significantly from firm to firm. However, the final decision should not be based on price alone.

GETTING THE BEST OUT OF YOUR SURVEYOR

There are two things that you should do in order to ensure that you get full value out of your survey report.

The first is to let the surveyor know about any specific concerns that you have about the property (e.g. a crack in the wall or a wonky door frame). This must be done before his visit. This will ensure that you get the necessary reassurance or otherwise.

The second thing is to send the surveyor particulars of any other properties that are for sale or recently sold in the area. The more comparables a surveyor has available, the more accurate will be his valuation. This is particularly important if you are using a surveyor from out of the area.

INTERPRETING THE REPORT

The surveyor's job is to point out every defect with the property. If he does not, he might be sued for negligence. Consequently a survey report can make even a nice property sound to be in quite poor condition. Generally speaking the surveyor's comments can be divided into one of three categories:

Urgent matters

These are defects that are judged to be an actual or developing threat to the fabric of the building or to personal safety. Such defects will have to be rectified immediately and may affect your decision to proceed with the purchase.

Significant matters

These are defects that you would not necessarily see for yourself and which might affect the price that you are prepared to pay for the property.

Observations

These are things that you could reasonably have been expected to see for yourself. For example, the kitchen is old-fashioned or the window frames need redecorating. The surveyor has to include such observations in his report to cover himself but you are unlikely to be able to use the existence of such defects to renegotiate the price.

If you are in any doubt about the seriousness of any defect you should not hesitate to phone the surveyor and ask for clarification. Most will be pleased to hear from you and may well be a lot more forthcoming 'off the record' than they were in writing.

INTERPRETING THE VALUATION

Surveyors' valuations tend to err on the side of caution and it is not uncommon to find that the valuation for mortgage purposes is less than the purchase price that has been agreed.

However, if the difference is more than about 5%, it could be that the price that you have agreed to pay is too high. In such cases the best thing to do is to telephone the surveyor and ask how he arrived at his valuation. If he persuades you that you have agreed to pay too much it may be necessary to renegotiate the purchase price (see page 124).

Case study

James McL and his wife Oonagh bought a four-bed-room Victorian property near Leeds for £250,000 with a £100,000 mortgage. They relied entirely on the mortgage valuation and did not instruct a surveyor of their own. On moving into the property James and Oonagh found that it was riddled with problems. There was damp in their daughter's bedroom caused by a leaking roof. There was damp in the kitchen caused by a defective damp course. The wiring was lethal and seemed to blow a fuse most days. The heating and plumbing seemed to have been installed by someone who was drunk and blind as well as incompetent. In total James and Oonagh spent £25,000 putting things right.

James rang his mortgage lender and complained that the surveyor who had carried out the mortgage valuation was incompetent. The lender explained that the surveyor's job was only to confirm that the property was satisfactory security for the £100,000 advance which was secured upon it. The surveyor had no duty of care to James and Oonagh.

Commenting on his experience James said 'I assumed that the building society surveyor would survey the property. I had no idea that his inspection would be so cursory. I really feel that the lender should have advised me to instruct my own surveyor. I shall certainly do so next time.'

Case study

Anne G and her husband Hamish bought a large house in rural Devon for £250,000. In addition to the mortgage valuation they commissioned a full building survey which revealed a number of expensive problems. The roof had been re-covered with the wrong tiles. The new ones were too heavy. They had caused serious structural damage and would have to be replaced. The electrical system was in urgent need of renewal. Worst of all the septic tank in the garden was leaking. The total cost of the repairs came to nearly £30,000.

Anne and Hamish showed the report to the seller and asked for a reduction of £30,000 from the asking price. The owner accepted that the repairs were necessary and after a couple of rounds of negotiation a revised price of £225,000 was agreed.

Commenting on her experiences Anne said 'Our survey seemed expensive at the time but it paid for itself many times over. It really proved to be an excellent investment'.

Case study

Samantha B agreed to buy a two-bedroom maisonette near Romford in Essex for £65,000. She instructed her mortgage lender to undertake a combined mortgage valuation and home buyer's report and used the surveyor who they recommended, who was based 35 miles away.

To her great disappointment the property was down-valued on survey to £62,000. She asked the vendor to reduce the sale price but he would not budge. She withdrew from the purchase and started to look at alternative properties.

A week later she had not found anything nearly as nice as the original flat so she rang the agent to say that she would like to proceed with the purchase after all. 'Too late,' the agent said. 'I have already found another buyer, at £66,000 this time.'

Samantha eventually bought an identical property further down the road. She paid £66,500 for it.

Commenting on her experience Samantha said 'With hindsight it is clear that the surveyor's valuation of £62,000 was wrong. It was simply not possible to buy a flat in that road for that price. The second time I instructed a local surveyor and had no problems with the valuation. But I ended up paying £1,500 more than I need have done. I am cross about the whole thing. I should have relied on my own instincts and proceeded with the original purchase'.

Case study
Mary P bought a two-bedroom garden flat in Hampstead, north London. She commissioned a home buyer's report which showed that the property was damp along the whole of the front wall.

The surveyor advised a specialist damp report. The damp report said that the damp course was defective and needed replacing. The plaster in both front rooms and the hallway would also need to be replaced. The total estimate was £4,000.

Mary decided to proceed with her purchase regardless. However, before undertaking the work she asked a local builder to give her a second opinion on the dampness. His conclusion was very different. He pointed out that the gravel drive was above the level of the damp course in several places. He felt that this was the likely cause of the damp.

Two days with a shovel and the problem was cured. By the summer the wall had dried out entirely. Mary covered up the discoloured plaster with some thick wallpaper and a proprietary sealant and spent the £3,500 that she had saved on a new car.

(10)

Consolidating the Sale

The present home-buying process is horribly inefficient. The average time taken between the offer being agreed and the exchange of contracts is 12 weeks and approximately 30% of all the sales that are agreed fail to reach completion. This chapter will explain how to speed the process up and increase the chance of a satisfactory completion.

HOW TO BUILD A GOOD RELATIONSHIP WITH THE VENDOR

Love him or loathe him you will have to try to maintain a satisfactory working relationship with your vendor until the sale reaches completion. The following hints will help you to do so:

Confirm everything in writing

A great many problems are caused by misunderstandings. As soon as your offer is accepted, you should write to the agent to confirm all the details and conditions of the sale. A typical letter might look like the example shown in Figure 9.

The agent should also confirm to you details of the sale in writing. Be sure to check this letter carefully to make sure that there are no discrepancies with what you have previously agreed.

Dear Mr Jones,

Re: 1 Park Avenue, Anytown
SUBJECT TO CONTRACT

Further to my telephone conversation with the agent this morning I was delighted to hear that my offer to purchase the above property for the sum of £69,500 subject to contract has been accepted. I confirm the following details:

1. My offer is to include all carpets and all curtains on the ground-floor rooms.

2. My offer is subject to the property being taken off the market immediately.

3. I am hoping to be able to exchange contracts within six weeks. My target completion date is 1 December.

4. I am applying for a 75% mortgage with the ABC Building Society. This is being arranged by XYZ Mortgage Brokers Limited, telephone no. 12345 679010.

5. I shall be arranging for a home buyer's survey on the property.

6. My solicitor is Mr G O Quickly, of Quickly and Company Solicitors, address plus telephone number.

7. I have agreed a sale on my current property. My buyer, who is buying for the first time, has already carried out a survey and the result is satisfactory. The agent handling the sale is Mr Ivor Sale, of Sale and Company, address and telephone number.

8. I can be contacted if necessary on 123456 daytime and 7891011 evenings.

I hope this is an accurate summary of our agreement and I look forward to the purchase proceeding quickly and smoothly.

Yours sincerely,

A Buyer

Figure 9. Letter confirming the details agreed
verbally with the vendor.

Arrange a consolidation visit

Last time you met the vendor you were adversaries. An excellent way to consolidate the sale is often to arrange to meet the vendor again in less adversarial circumstances. The best bet is to think of a pretext which allows you to visit the property again, e.g. to measure for curtains or carpets. If you have a family, take them with you. During the visit tell the vendors how much you are looking forward to moving in and talk positively about what you are doing to expedite matters. The psychology behind this is that if you can establish a cordial relationship at the outset, you will be much better placed to resolve any difficulties that may arise later on.

Give regular progress reports

It is vital to keep your vendor fully informed of all progress. Let them know as soon as you have a date for a survey, as soon as you receive a satisfactory survey result, as soon as you receive a mortgage and whenever else a significant event occurs. In any event try to keep in touch at least once a week. It is usually best to keep in touch with the estate agent rather than the vendors themselves unless you get on exceptionally well.

If a problem occurs, let the agent and/or the vendor know immediately. This will help to create an atmosphere of two parties who are working together to achieve a satisfactory outcome. It will also help to ensure that more time is available to resolve the issue.

The importance of speed

Above all else you need to exchange contracts as quickly as possible. There is a direct correlation between the length of time that the sale takes and the chances of it falling through. Every day of unnecessary delay is another day when things could go wrong. With this in mind I devote most of the rest of this chapter to suggesting some things that you can do to speed matters up.

TEN WAYS TO GET A QUICKER MORTGAGE OFFER

1. **Choice of mortgage lender** – choose your mortgage lender with care. The time it takes to deal with a mortgage application varies considerably from one lender to another. The quickest can give you a mortgage offer in ten days. The slowest often take four to six weeks. Check with your mortgage broker how long the mortgage offer is likely to take. If you are arranging a mortgage direct with the lender ask them what their average turnaround is before you commit yourself.

2. **Apply for a mortgage in principle** – if you know which mortgage lender you wish to use you can often apply for a mortgage in principle before you find a property to buy. This means that the mortgage lender will take up employment and financial references and give you a certificate to say that they will lend you up to £X,000 subject to a satisfactory valuation on the property that you are buying. This can save seven to 14 days once you find a property (NB not all lenders offer a mortgage in principle).

3. **Ask for the survey to be done first** – most mortgage lenders will not instruct the surveyor to carry out a mortgage valuation until they have obtained satisfac-

tory financial and employment references. The reason for this is that they want to avoid wasting your survey fee if you are not creditworthy. The price however is a delay of seven to ten days.

The way to avoid this is to instruct the mortgage lender to proceed with the survey before obtaining references. This will usually have to be done in writing. A typical letter would read:

Dear XYZ Building Society,

Re: 1 Park Avenue, Anytown

I am in a hurry to buy this property. In order to save time, I should be grateful if you would instruct the surveyor immediately, i.e. *before* obtaining references. I understand that if my references are not satisfactory, I will lose my survey fee but I am prepared to take this risk in order to obtain an early mortgage offer.

Yours sincerely,

A Buyer

Figure 10. Letter requesting a building society
to proceed with a survey before obtaining references.

4. **Inform your employer** – mortgage applications are often delayed because employers are slow to respond, or respond to a reference request incorrectly. Find out which person in your organisation will be dealing with the reference and ensure that the lender sends it addressed to them by name. Go and see this person and ask them to look out for the reference and return it immediately. Also make sure that they complete the

mortgage lender's official reference request form. Most lenders will not accept the information in letter form.

5. **Check the lender's lending criteria** – many mortgages are turned down because the property does not meet the lender's criteria. If you are applying direct to the lender or if your broker is not a mortgage specialist ask for a copy of the lender's lending criteria and check that the property that you are buying falls within them.

6. **Do your own credit check** – if there is any possibility that you have a County Court Judgement for debt, ask your mortgage broker to do a credit check on you. If there is a problem, you can save the time that would be wasted if your loan application was refused and apply in the first case to a more appropriate mortgage lender.

7. **Choose the right surveyor** – before instructing a surveyor make sure that you ask how quickly they can get the report to you. Sometimes a surveyor will agree to do a report for you quickly in return for a higher fee.

8. **Stress the urgency** – mortgage lenders have been known to deal with applications within 48 hours. If you tell everyone that you are in a hurry, you might be surprised at what they can do to help.

9. **Check if a medical report is required** – most people who are arranging a mortgage will be applying for

some sort of life assurance policy to cover the loan. If the loan is a large one (about £100,000 plus) or if you have ever had any medical problems, the insurance company might ask for a medical report. This could cause one to two weeks delay. If there is any possibility that your insurer may require a medical report, ring their underwriting department, and explain your circumstances. If a report is required, it can be arranged immediately. If you are arranging your loan through a broker he will usually do this for you.

10. **Hassle people** – as the saying goes, the squeaky wheel gets the grease. If promised deadlines are not met, don't be frightened to complain loudly.

THREE WAYS TO SAVE TIME ON THE LEGAL SIDE

1. **Choose the right solicitor** – I cannot over-emphasise the importance of choosing the right solicitor. Get recommendations from your friends, the estate agent, the mortgage broker and the lending source. Speak to more than one firm before making a decision and never choose on price alone.

2. **Instruct a solicitor as early as possible** – if you are selling a property as well as buying, you should instruct a solicitor *before* you find a buyer. This will allow the solicitor to obtain the Title Deeds, prepare a draft contract, and prepare replies to standard pre-contract enquiries in readiness for the sale. This will save time once a buyer is found.

3. **Check what costs are involved** – a great many sales fall

through because the buyer underestimates the cost involved. However, do check with your solicitor that the costs that you allowed for are accurate in your case.

Case study

The flat that Marilyn P bought was an absolute bargain. The vendor, who was emigrating to New Zealand, had just lost a sale and was in a desperate hurry to sell quickly. He agreed to accept Marilyn's price provided that she could exchange contracts within 21 days.

Marilyn applied for a mortgage with the ABC Bank which her broker assured her had a reputation for swift service. She gave the bank written authority to go to survey before taking up references and by ringing around, she found a surveyor who could visit the flat the following day. Her broker told the bank that she was in a hurry and they pulled out all the stops. Five days later she had an offer of a mortgage.

Marilyn's solicitor was equally efficient. He came highly recommended and more than lived up to his reputation. Eleven days later Marilyn exchanged contracts.

Commenting on her experiences Marilyn said 'I spent hours running about to get everything done quickly, but it was certainly worth it. I love my new flat and I got it at an excellent price'.

(11)

When Things Go Wrong

Under the present home-buying system one in three of all sales fails to reach completion. By following the advice given in previous chapters, you will significantly reduce the odds of your purchase going wrong. However, there is nothing that can be done to guarantee that your purchase will be trouble-free. In this chapter I will describe some of the more common problems which you may experience and give advice on how to resolve them.

HOW TO AVOID BEING GAZUMPED
Of all the things that can go wrong gazumping is the one that raises the fiercest passions.

What is gazumping?
Lets start by getting the definition right. Gazumping means a vendor reneging on his agreement to sell you a property at a certain price. For example, a property is for sale at an asking price of £99,950. You make an offer of £95,000 which the vendor accepts. A few hours, days or even weeks later, a second buyer makes an offer of £96,000 for the same property. The vendor rings you and says:

A. I'm selling to someone else for more money or
B. Unless you increase your offer to £96,000 or more I will sell to somebody else.

In both cases you have been gazumped.

Gazumping is *not* the acceptance of an offer above the asking price. In order to gazump you a vendor has to renege on an offer after it has been accepted. Thus, if a property is for sale at £99,950 and two buyers bid against each other until a sale is agreed at £105,000 the losing party has not been gazumped. They have just been outbid.

How common is gazumping?

Gazumping is not nearly as common as the press would have us believe. It affects only about 1–2% of all transactions and occurs mostly in London and the south east where the market is most buoyant. Nevertheless, when it does occur, it is most unpleasant. The gazumped buyer is caused considerable inconvenience and is often left with a bill for legal fees and survey fees of several hundred pounds.

Why does it happen?

Gazumping usually occurs because a property is kept on the market after a sale has been agreed. Sometimes there is a legitimate reason for the vendor to do this. For example, the buyer has not yet sold their own property. In other cases, the vendor is dissatisfied with the original offer and keeps the property on the market in order to try to obtain a higher one.

Gazumping is most likely to happen when a sale is slow to progress in a buoyant market. In a buoyant market, prices can sometimes rise by as much as 2–3% per month. Thus a property that is sold for £100,000 could be worth as much as £109,000 by the time a slow purchaser is ready to exchange contracts 12 weeks later.

Whose fault is it?

Estate agents are usually held responsible for gazumping. In truth, they are not usually the guilty party. An estate agent has a legal and ethical duty to act in accordance with his client's instructions at all times. Thus, if a client tells him to keep the property on the market after an offer has been accepted, then he must do so. If a higher offer is received, the agent must by law pass it on to the vendor. The decision to gazump someone is always made by the vendor not by the agent. The real culprit though is the outdated home-buying process which causes an average delay of eight weeks before contracts can be exchanged.

How can you avoid being gazumped?

There are five things you can do to reduce the chances of being gazumped:

♦ Do not try to buy a property until you have sold your own.

♦ Insist that the property you are buying is taken off the market as a condition of your offer.

♦ Exchange contracts as quickly as possible.

♦ Keep the vendor closely informed of all progress.

♦ Try to maintain a cordial relationship with the vendor throughout.

THE VENDOR WHO NO LONGER WANTS TO SELL

A simple change of mind by either party is the single most

common cause of sales falling through. However, it is comparatively rare for someone to change their mind for no reason at all. The way to deal with a vendor who changes their mind about selling to you is to find out why they have changed their mind. Ask the estate agent *why* the vendor has changed his mind. If you can't get a satisfactory answer, try ringing the vendor yourself. Very often you will find that the reason that they have changed their mind is because their mortgage application was turned down or they received an adverse survey report on the property that they were buying. If you can find out what the real problem is you may be able to solve it.

LATE SURVEY

The survey should be carried out within 10 to 14 days of submitting the mortgage application. It is important that the survey is carried out promptly because it is the first sign the vendor has that your mortgage application is proceeding. If the survey is late, the most likely reason is a problem with your financial or employment references. The other possibility is inefficiency on behalf of the lender and/or the surveyor.

The best way to avoid delays here is to ask the surveyor to commit to a date when he will be able to carry out the survey and a date when he will be able to submit the final report *before* you instruct him. If the survey is not carried out on this date, you can telephone to complain. If the surveyor cannot carry out the survey within a satisfactory timescale your last resort is to cancel your instructions and instruct another (less busy) surveyor.

DOWN-VALUATION ON SURVEY

It is quite common to find that the surveyor's valuation for mortgage purposes is less than the agreed purchase price. There are several things that you can do to avoid this problem from occurring.

♦ Instruct a surveyor with up-to-date knowledge of local values.

♦ Provide the surveyor with particulars of any comparable properties which you have relied upon to form your own opinion of value.

♦ Choose your surveyor with care – some have a reputation for over-cautious valuation.

♦ If you are applying for a high percentage mortgage, let the surveyor know that the valuation is critical at the time that you instruct him.

If despite these precautions the property is still down-valued, you will have to make a decision on whether you are able to and/or still wish to proceed.

Can you afford to proceed

If you are applying for a 95% mortgage from a lender that will not lend more than 95% of the purchase price, any down-valuation will mean that you will have to find money from elsewhere in order to increase your deposit. For example:

Agreed price	£100,000
95% mortgage advance	£95,000
Deposit required	£5,000

Surveyor values property at	£95,000
Maximum advance is therefore	
95% × £95,000	£90,250
Deposit required	£9,750

You may be able to persuade your vendor to accept a corresponding reduction in the purchase price. If not, unless you can find another £4,750 you will not be able to proceed.

You may be able to arrange a top-up loan from another source but this is likely to be expensive. However, some mortgage lenders will not allow you to borrow the further money elsewhere for fear that it may compromise their security. If you still want to proceed with your purchase, the only alternative is to apply to another mortgage lender and hope that a different surveyor values the property at the full purchase price.

If the mortgage that you are applying for is below the lender's maximum loan to valuation you will not have to find the extra money in cash. The lender will simply increase the percentage loan. For example:

Purchase Price	£100,000
Loan	£70,000
Deposit	£30,000
Loan to valuation ratio is	70%
Property valued at	£90,000
Loan	£70,000

Loan to valuation is
£70,000 ÷ £90,000   77.7%

A point to bear in mind is that in this example, the new
loan is above 75% of the valuation. This means that some
lenders would charge a mortgage indemnity premium (see
Chapter 2). This could increase the cost of the loan by
several hundred pounds.

Do you still want to proceed?

Once you have determined whether you can afford to
proceed, you have to decide whether you still wish to do
so. The first thing to do is to make your own value
judgement. Do you still think the property is worth the
purchase price agreed? Having decided this, your exact
course of action will depend upon a number of factors.

If you are buying a highly desirable property in a buoyant
market and you believe the property to be worth the price
agreed, the best course of action might be to proceed
without mentioning the down-valuation to the vendor.
Your chance of securing a price reduction may be slight
and any attempt to do so could jeopardise your purchase.

If the property is less desirable or the market less buoyant,
you might want to use the survey report to try to negotiate
a reduction in the purchase price. If so, it is well worth
telephoning the surveyor and asking him how he arrived
at his valuation. You can use these arguments to support
your case. It is usually best to handle these negotiations in
writing. A typical letter is shown in Figure 11.

Dear Mr Jones,

Re: 1 Park Avenue, Anytown
SUBJECT TO CONTRACT

I am sorry to inform you that my surveyor has valued the property at £90,000. This is £10,000 less than the agreed purchase price. I am enclosing a copy of the report. I have challenged my surveyor over his valuation but he has defended it by citing several comparable properties particularly No. 7 which has just been sold for £90,000.

In the light of this I feel that I must revise my offer to £90,000. I still hope that the sale will be able to continue and I look forward to hearing from you with your comments.

Yours sincerely,

A Buyer

Figure 11. Letter querying a valuation.

If the vendor refuses to budge at all or if he is prepared to concede only part of the differential, you will have to make a decision on whether to proceed or not. Your decision should be based not on the surveyor's valuation but on how easy it will be to buy a similar property for the same or a lower amount. You should also consider the amount of inconvenience that you would suffer if you withdrew from the purchase.

If you do withdraw, always leave the door open for the future. It is surprising how many vendors call your bluff then call back 24 hours later and say that they will accept the lower offer after all. You need to make it easy for your vendor to do this without losing face. A typical withdrawal letter is shown in Figure 12.

Dear Mr Jones,

Re: 1 Park Avenue, Anytown,
SUBJECT TO CONTRACT

I am so sorry that we were unable to reach an agreement on a revised purchase price. For the reasons stated I am not prepared to pay more than £92,500. I am now looking for an alternative property but I should like to buy yours. Please let me know if you change your mind.

Yours sincerely,

A Buyer

Figure 12. Letter withdrawing an offer.

SURVEY REVEALS REPAIRS NEEDED

If the survey reveals repairs are needed, you will need to renegotiate the purchase price using similar principles to those set out above. Before you quantify your request you will need to separate the work highlighted in the survey into three separate categories:

- Faults that have been allowed for in the price.
- Faults that you could have spotted yourself.
- Faults that you could not have spotted yourself.

If the need to replace the roof was discussed before the offer was made you can hardly expect the vendor to agree to another reduction to reflect the cost of this. If you complain that the windows need painting, the vendor may reasonably point out that you could have noticed this for yourself and allowed for it in your original offer. The third category of faults may warrant a reduction.

Before you make a request for a reduction you need to make sure that you have an accurate idea of the likely cost of the necessary work. For this you cannot rely on the survey report. Most surveyors are general practice surveyors. This means that they can identify most faults but will not necessarily have an up-to-date idea of the cost of rectifying them. If the work required is extensive, it may be worth getting a builder's estimate before you commence negotiations. If the work required is very extensive you may need to commission a quantity surveyor to prepare a detailed estimate.

It is usually best to make you request for a reduction in writing. Here is a typical letter.

Dear Mr Jones,

Re: 1 Park Avenue, Anytown
SUBJECT TO CONTRACT

I have just received my survey report which I am afraid has revealed a number of problems:

♦ The damp course needs replacing, estimated cost £2,500.
♦ The garden wall is dangerous and needs rebuilding, estimated cost £1,000.
♦ The heating system does not function properly, estimated cost £2,000.

All the above matters require urgent attention and in view of this I must reduce my offer from £95,000 to £90,000 to reflect the cost of the work.
I still very much want to proceed with my purchase and I hope that this revised offer will be acceptable to you.

I am enclosing a copy of my survey report.

Yours sincerely,

A Buyer

Figure 13. Letter requesting a reduction in the price.

If the vendor will not agree to reduce by the whole amount, you will need to take a decision on whether or not to proceed. As before, this decision should take into account the ease with which you are likely to be able to find an alternative property and the inconvenience that pulling out of the sale would cause to you and your family.

Retention notices

If a defect is minor, the surveyor will merely point it out. If the defect is more serious, the lender may ask you to give an undertaking that you will complete the necessary repairs within say six months. In practice mortgage lenders seldom check to see whether you have actually done so.

If the defect is very serious, the lender may make a 'retention'. This means that they will retain a certain sum until the repairs have been carried out. The problem is that if the lender retains £5,000 to cover the cost of fixing the roof, where do you get the money from to fix the roof?

The solution is to go to your own bank and arrange a short-term loan. The bank may require an undertaking from your solicitor to repay the loan out of the mortgage advance when it is released. This type of loan is fairly easy to arrange but it will take a week or two to organise and this could cause delay.

The way to avoid this is to ring the mortgage lender a day or two after the survey took place and ask if the surveyor has found any major defects. If he did, you need to ask whether they intend to make a retention. By making this phone call, you will find out about the problem sooner and have more time to arrange a temporary loan.

Total retention
When the defect is very serious, the lender may retain the entire mortgage advance until repairs have been completed. The process for dealing with this is described above. However, a larger loan will take longer to arrange.

Damp reports
The surveyor will often ask for a damp report. The way to prevent this from causing delay is to telephone the surveyor the day after he has visited the property. Ask if there are any major problems and whether he will be asking for any supplementary reports.

If he has recommended a damp report, you will have extra time to arrange one. The estate agent will probably be able to recommend a company who can carry out a report. For the reasons stated in Chapter 9, you should treat their recommendations with suspicion.

Timber report
If the property that you are buying is an older one and does not have current timber guarantees, the surveyor may ask for a timber report. The process for dealing with this is the same as for the damp report. Many companies undertake both damp and timber treatment and will produce a combined report.

Structural engineer's report
If the property shows any signs of subsidence or has a history of subsidence, the valuer may ask for a structural

engineer's report. Often this is just a precautionary measure. However, the consequences of subsidence can be so serious that many buyers run a mile at the mere mention of the word.

Having got this far it is probably worth paying for the structural engineer to visit the property before you pull out. His visit may entirely alleviate your fears. If the property does have subsidence it may prove extremely difficult to resell and even if your mortgage lender is prepared to lend on the property you should think carefully about proceeding.

UNINSURABLE PROPERTIES

If a property has ever suffered from subsidence or is in an area prone to flooding, it will be difficult to obtain buildings insurance even after the necessary repairs have been carried out. If you are buying such a property, the easiest solution is often to take over the current buildings policy from the present owner.

Be warned though. The cost of insurance may be much more than usual. You should therefore obtain a quote before committing yourself and possibly negotiate a reduction in the purchase price sufficient to compensate you for the high cost of future premiums.

DELAYED MORTGAGE OFFERS

One of the most common problems of all is delays in receiving the final mortgage offer. Until you have got this you cannot exchange contracts. This problem can be largely avoided by choosing a mortgage lender with a reputation for speed and efficiency of service. Unfortunately this may mean a trade-off with the mortgage rate. A mortgage lender that is offering a particularly attractive rate is likely to receive more applications than usual. This often leads to delays in underwriting cases. You will need to make your own decision on this but bear in mind that a mortgage that is a quarter of a per cent cheaper will be of little use to you if you end up losing the property that you are trying to buy.

All mortgage lenders experience peaks and troughs in the number of mortgage applications that they receive and you may just be unlucky or have applied during a particularly busy period. If you do not receive a mortgage offer within seven days of the survey being carried out you need to telephone the mortgage lender or your broker to find out whether there is a specific problem that is holding things up. If not, you need to find out the name of the person who is responsible for getting your mortgage offer out and badger them every day until you receive it.

MEDICAL REPORTS

If you are applying for any sort of life assurance policy as part of your mortgage application, the insurer may need a medical report. This usually happens when the policy applied for is particularly large (usually about £100,000 plus) or if there is anything adverse in your medical history (a close relative who has had a heart attack).

A medical report typically takes seven to ten days to arrange. If one is necessary, you need to know as soon as possible in order to avoid it causing an unnecessary delay.

If you suspect that a medical report may be required in your case ring the life assurance company and ask them.

LIFE COVER REFUSED

If your medical history is very poor, your life policy may be refused. In this case you need to approach a specialist independent insurance broker who has experience in impaired life cases. Even if your health is very poor most risks are insurable at a price. If your broker does not have the experience necessary to arrange such a policy ask him to recommend one who does.

Case study

Bill C agreed to buy a two-bedroom luxury flat in Bournemouth for £95,000. The vendor accepted Bill's offer but said that he would leave the property on the market just in case something went wrong. Three weeks later Bill received his survey report. The property had been down-valued to £90,000 due to the need to replace the old-fashioned kitchen and bathroom. Bill sent a copy of the survey to his vendor and asked for a £5,000 reduction in the purchase price.

His vendor responded with fury. Much of his reply is unrepeatable but the gist of it was that Bill could have seen the state of the kitchen and bathroom for himself, that the flat was worth £95,000 and that if Bill didn't want to buy it a queue of other people did.

Bill was a bit taken aback by this but on reflection decided that he did want to continue with his purchase. When he informed his vendor of this the following day he met with another barrage of abuse. Apparently the vendor had now agreed to sell to another party at £98,000 and was no longer prepared to consider Bill's offer.

Commenting on his experience Bill said 'I shall never know whether the vendor was intending to gazump me and use the survey report as an excuse or whether he reacted badly because he thought I was trying it on. With hindsight the flat was worth £95,000 and I wish I had not tried to negotiate a reduction. I shall almost certainly have to pay more for another flat like it'.

Case study

Stan B was buying a three-bedroom house in Swansea for his son who had just secured a university place there. The house was an ordinary house in a rather run-down part of the town but it was better and cheaper than student digs and Stan felt that it would be a good investment.

The property was down-valued on survey from £45,000 to £40,000 because of dampness, wiring problems and problems with the roof. Stan sent the agent a copy of his survey report together with a letter making a revised offer of £40,000. The vendor was reluctant to accept this.

Stan checked to make sure that similar properties were available then sent another letter to the agent mentioning that another property was now for sale in the road for £38,000 and basically saying that the vendor could take his offer or leave it. The vendor accepted the revised offer.

Commenting on his tactic Stan said 'I was in a strong negotiating position because I knew that I could walk away. There were plenty of other properties available, and the market was fairly stagnant. With hindsight I could probably have bought the house for £38,000'.

Case study

Hilary M made an offer to buy a two-bedroom Victorian cottage in south-east London. The property was in a terrible state but Hilary felt the price agreed reflected this. The survey revealed the problems that she had expected and valued the property at the full purchase price. However, in view of the severity of the problems, the lender said that it would hold back £30,000 of the £70,000 mortgage advance until the problems had been rectified.

On the advice of her mortgage broker Hilary went to her bank and negotiated a £30,000 loan to fund the shortfall. Her solicitor gave an undertaking to repay this out of the proceeds of the mortgage advance when it was released.

Commenting on her experience Hilary said 'When I read the mortgage offer and saw the £30,000 retention, I thought that was the end of it. Fortunately my broker knew what to do. I am delighted with my property and now the work is finished it is probably worth at least £20,000 more than I paid for it. It was an excellent buy.'

(12)

Legal Problems

There are so many legal problems that can occur during a property purchase that I have decided to give them a chapter all of their own. Here are 15 of the most common problems and how to overcome them. The recurrent theme is if you know what problems to expect, you can take action soon enough to avoid or resolve them. If the problems are not uncovered until a few days before exchange of contracts is due to take place, it may be too late to do anything about them.

1. Slow/pedantic solicitor
I have already emphasised the importance of choosing a solicitor with care. Once you have chosen a solicitor it is extremely difficult to change to another one. By the time you had arranged for all the documents to be returned, you would have wasted at least seven to ten days. Changing solicitors halfway through is not to be recommended except in the most extreme of circumstances.

If your solicitor fails to live up to your expectations all you can do is to badger and cajole him into action. Never forget that you are the customer.

2. Delays in obtaining Title Deeds
The vendor's solicitor cannot prepare the draft contract until he has the Title Deeds. If the property that you are

buying is mortgaged, these will usually be held by the vendor's mortgage lender. If the vendor owns the property outright, the title deeds may be held for safe keeping by his previous mortgage lender, his bank or his solicitor. On the other hand they may have fallen down behind the piano.

It is reasonable to allow the vendor's solicitor seven to ten days to obtain the Title Deeds. Ask your solicitor or the estate agent to check that they have been obtained within this time scale. If not, you need to get the vendor to chase up his mortgage lender and/or his solicitor.

If the Deeds have been lost, the vendor will have to reconstruct his title to the property. This could cause considerable delay. In such cases you might do well to consider finding an alternative property.

3. Delays in obtaining office copy entries

If the property that you are buying has registered title, the vendor's solicitor will apply for office copy entries of the title from the Land Registry. These too must be obtained before the draft contract can be prepared. Some solicitors do not apply for office copy entries until a week or two into the sale in order to avoid incurring a fee if the sale fails to proceed for any reason. This will cause delays later on. Unless you have good cause to doubt whether the sale is going to proceed you should check with your solicitor that office copy entries have been requested during the first progress call.

4. Unregistered title

There are two systems of land conveyancing in England

and Wales. In the registered system, title to the land is registered at the Land Registry and guaranteed by the state. Disputes over title are therefore rare.

In the unregistered system, title is not registered with or guaranteed by the state. It must be proved by checking details of all previous conveyances. Disputes are therefore much more common and can become protracted. If you are buying an unregistered property and there is any dispute over the vendor's title, the best advice might be to abandon your purchase and seek an alternative property.

5. Delays in receiving draft contracts

Your solicitor should receive a draft contract within a couple of weeks. If he has not, you need to investigate the cause of the delay. It could be that the vendor's solicitor is waiting for the Title Deeds or office copy entries. It could be that he has all the necessary documents but has been slow to produce the contract. In either event you should ring the agent or the vendor and ask them to chivvy things along.

6. Disputes over the terms of contract

The draft contract is the document that sets out the terms of the sale. Most of the clauses are standard or semi-standard and come straight from a word processor. These are seldom contentious. The problem arises when a non-standard clause is introduced and its inclusion or exclusion turns into a battle of wills between the solicitors.

If you were told that your purchase is being held up due to difficulty in agreeing the terms of the contract, you should insist that your solicitor explains in layman's terms what the relevant clause covers and what the dispute is about. Very often a quick chat with the vendor or his agent will facilitate resolution of the problem.

7. Delays in obtaining local searches

Some local authorities are notoriously slow at responding to search enquiries. In order to avoid delays later on, it is essential to check that your solicitor has applied for a search immediately. However, often even this isn't soon enough and the absence of a local search ends up being the only thing that prevents contracts being exchanged.

In such circumstances the best solution might be to arrange a personal search. This means that someone (a member of staff from your own solicitors or a professional search agent) will visit the council in person to obtain the information that the council is too busy to provide. You will have to pay for the time involved. You will also have to buy an insurance policy to protect against the consequences of anything being missed. The total cost might be three or four times as much as the usual search fee but it is worth it if prevents you from losing your property.

8. Delays in answering preliminary enquiries

Your solicitor will submit a long list of questions to the vendor's solicitor. These questions will cover issues such as:

◆ Boundaries and any disputes relating to them.
◆ Covenants and easements.

- Mains services.
- Guarantees for work carried out.
- NHBC certificate if the property is new.
- Planning matters.
- Fixtures and fittings.

The full list of questions looks quite intimidating but in fact many of the questions are standard and many of the answers are 'I do not know' or 'Rely upon your own enquiries'. If there is a delay in providing this information you will need to check whether the vendor has failed to supply the necessary information or whether the solicitor has not passed it on. Some questions tend to cause a disproportionate amount of problems (see next four sections).

9. Boundary disputes

If your vendor has ever had a dispute over boundaries or fences with any of their neighbours your solicitor will probably advise you to run a mile. The consequences of a boundary dispute are regularly featured in television *Neighbours from Hell* documentaries. One of the worst cases I know involved a farmer and his neighbour in Oxfordshire who were arguing over a strip of land 18 inches wide and 90 feet long. Between them they ran up legal costs of over £100,000.

The farmer lost and ended up forfeiting the land and paying the legal costs of both sides. For the same sum, the farmer could have bought about thirty acres of land anywhere else in Oxfordshire.

The new Land Registration Act which came into force in October 2003 should make it easier for landowners in England and Wales to register precise boundary lines around their properties, to prevent future disputes. The new act also stipulates that an independent adjudicator will have the power to rule on individual disputes.

It remains to be seen how well the new act will work in practice. For the time being if you are determined to proceed with the purchase regardless, you would be well advised to try to meet the neighbour concerned yourself in order to try to ensure that the dispute does not reoccur in the future.

10. Restrictive covenants
Restrictive covenants fall into two categories, those that have already been broken, and those that have not. For example, suppose that you are buying a five-year-old property on an estate. The builder may have put a covenant on all properties that forbids the addition of any extensions without his approval. The reason for this is to ensure that the estate is not disfigured by ugly extensions.

If you are planning to add a conservatory after you buy the property, you would have to approach the developer to ask permission. Most developers charge an administration fee to consider your application. If it is rejected, you would have to take a view on whether you still wished to proceed with the purchase.

Much more serious problems are caused when a covenant has already been breached. Let's suppose that you are buying a Victorian property with the same covenant preventing extensions being built. However, in this instance an extension has already been added to the property. It might be impossible to track down the developer who built the house a hundred years ago to ask for his permission retrospectively. However, there is a risk that his successors could at some future time try to enforce the covenant. If they did, it may mean demolition of the extension. The solution to this type of problem is to buy an insurance policy that protects against the risk of loss should a covenant be enforced. Because the risk of most covenants being enforced is slight, premiums tend to be relatively modest. It normally takes a couple of weeks to arrange such a policy.

11. Planning and building regulation problems

If the property that you are buying has an extension added, your solicitor will need to check that it has the appropriate planning and building regulation consents.

If it has not, it may be necessary to apply for these retrospectively. This could cause lengthy delays. Indeed, the council might refuse to give consent and insist that the extension in question is demolished. If you run into problems of this nature, it may be best to look for another property.

The way to avoid such problems is to ask the owner or their estate agent three questions *before* you make an offer:

◆ Have you ever added an extension to the property?

- If so did you apply for planning consent?
- Did you get building regulation approval?

Asking these questions at the outset could save a great deal of time, money and frustration later on.

12. Disputes over fixtures and fittings

Fixtures and fittings cause more arguments than anything else. I know of many cases where an argument over a washing line, a toothbrush holder or quarter of a tank of heating oil has jeopardised a sale. Don't let it happen to you. A detailed list of what is and is not included should be agreed in writing through the estate agents at the time that the offer is agreed and confirmed by the solicitors. If a dispute over a trivial item does blow up don't be bloody minded. It may be humiliating to let your vendor get away with digging up the rose bush in the front garden but it is not worth pulling out of the sale over.

13. Insufficient funds to exchange

Many purchasers underestimate the costs that they will incur when buying a property. Make sure that you obtain a detailed estimate of all the costs that you will incur on day one. Your estate agent, mortgage broker or solicitor will all be pleased to do this for you.

A particular problem occurs when buyers are obtaining a mortgage for more than 90% of the purchase price. In such circumstances most solicitors will accept a reduced deposit on exchange of contracts but some will not. If this is the case, you will need to know as soon as possible so that you can arrange an alternative loan for the balance.

Finally remember that your solicitor will not exchange contracts until the cheque that you give him to fund the deposit has cleared. Either arrange a bankers draft or ensure that your solicitor has your cheque at least seven days before the exchange of contracts is due to occur.

14. Use of deposit by vendor
Most solicitors will allow the purchaser deposit to be passed up the chain to fund the vendor's own purchase.

However some solicitors won't allow their client's deposit to be used in this way because there is a small risk that it could be lost. The way to avoid problems here is to ask your solicitor early on in the sale whether he will allow your deposit to be used to fund the vendor's deposit on their purchase. If not, you need to warn your vendor about this in good time so that he can make alternative arrangements.

15. Arguments over completion dates
Many chains break down because the parties involved cannot agree on a completion date. There are three things that you can do to avoid problems here. The first is to let everyone know your target completion from the very outset. The second is to be aware that completion dates do not have to be 28 days. They can be as short or as long as the parties wish them to be. Sometimes a simultaneous exchange and completion suits everyone best. On other occasions, an extended completion period of perhaps three or six months can give all parties the best combination of early certainty and sufficient time to make their personal arrangements.

Finally, don't dismiss the option of moving into temporary accommodation or even taking a bridging loan. If contracts have been exchanged, the risk of things going wrong is very slight. The cost of moving twice might be less than the cost of withdrawing from the purchase.

SPECIAL PROBLEMS WITH LEASEHOLD PROPERTIES

It would take a whole book to cover all the problems that can affect leasehold properties. However I shall cover the most common three here:

1. Short lease

If the lease has less than about 70 years left to run, you may have difficulty in reselling the property (except in central London). If you are buying such a property, it is a sensible precaution to enquire about the cost of buying a lease extension as early as possible in the transaction. If the cost is prohibitive, you may wish to reconsider your decision to proceed with purchase.

New legislation which came into effect in October 2003 does now give certain leaseholders the right to buy their own freehold at a 'fair price' but the legislation is complex and you will need to check with your solicitor to ensure that it applies to the property that you are buying before you proceed further.

2. Defective lease

A lot of the flats that were converted from large houses during the 1970s and 80s suffer from badly drafted leases. A typical problem would be failure to define clearly who is responsible for maintaining the common parts. If the defect in the lease is serious, your solicitor might advise you not to proceed unless you are able to obtain a Deed 'of Variation'. This means getting the freeholder's permission to change the original terms of the lease. Negotiations over this could become quite protracted and there is no guarantee of success. If you are in a hurry to buy the best thing might be to find another property.

3. Unpaid service charges

Responsibility for maintaining the building often rests with the landlord. Some landlords collect substantial service charges every year but fail to carry out any maintenance work. In such circumstances leaseholders sometimes stop paying the service charge. This is most unwise. The law in this area is very one-sided. It is extremely difficult for leaseholders to force their landlords to undertake maintenance work but the sanctions that landlords can employ against leaseholders who fail to pay their service charges are draconian.

However unfair it may seem, your vendor will have to pay all charges up to date before they can sell their flat. If the landlord has a very poor history of maintaining the building, you may wish to reconsider your decision to buy the property.

New legislation does now give certain leaseholders the right to take over the management of their block but the legislation is complex and you will need to check with your solicitor to ensure that it applies to the property that you are buying before you proceed further.

PROBLEMS WITH THE CHAIN

All the problems highlighted in this section can also affect other people up and down the chain. If you suspect this to be the case, you may have to do a little detective work of your own by ringing other agents, purchasers or vendors to establish what the problem is.

Case study

The present owner of the property Petra K was buying had built a small extension onto his kitchen nine months ago. The extension was so small that planning permission had not been required. Unfortunately the extension still needed building regulation approval and the vendor had failed to apply for this.

The first that Petra knew of the problem was when her solicitor received replies to preliminary enquiries. Petra's solicitor warned her to abandon her purchase at that point, but as it was such a pretty cottage she did not want to give up without a fight.

The vendor applied to the council for retrospective approval. They said the building inspectors would look at the extension and the building inspector made pages of notes about items that might not comply with current regulations. The correspondence went back and forwards for 14 weeks until the council was eventually satisfied. In the meanwhile Petra was forced to take unpleasant and temporary accommodation.

Commenting on her experience Petra said 'With hindsight I should have taken my solicitor's advice; withdrawn as soon as the problem arose. I have been put to considerable inconvenience but let's look on the bright side – at least I got the property in the end. I might have waited 14 weeks only to find that the council insisted on demolishing half the kitchen'.

Case study

Martin S had been unhappy with his solicitors almost from the outset. The nice chap who gave him the quote was always too busy to speak to him and he had little confidence in his assistant. The final straw came two days before exchange of contracts was due to take place. Martin's solicitor rang to tell him that his vendor's solicitor would not take a reduced deposit. Martin would have to find another £5,000 before he could exchange.

Martin was furious. Surely this problem could have been discovered weeks ago. Why had it not been mentioned before? His solicitor could give no satisfactory explanation.

Fortunately Martin was able to arrange a bank loan for the balance but it cost him nearly £200 and it delayed exchange of contracts for a week. His vendor was furious and he nearly lost the property.

Commenting on his experience Martin said 'This problem could easily have been predicted. I am still cross that I was not told about the problems sooner. I shall certainly not use that firm of solicitors again'.

(13)

Preparing for the Move

This chapter will explain what you need to do in order to ensure that the move itself goes smoothly.

PREPARING FOR EXCHANGE OF CONTRACTS

You will know that exchange of contracts is imminent when your solicitor asks to arrange an appointment to sign the contract. Although this is certainly a good sign you would do well not to relax just yet. Things can and do go wrong at the very last minute. Two problems in particular arise more often than most.

Arguments over completion dates

Even at this late stage sales can and do break down because the parties involved are unable to agree on a completion date. The things that you can do to defuse this problem were explained in the last chapter.

Gazumping

A really heartless vendor may try to gazump you on the very day that you are due to exchange contracts. He knows that at this point you will have invested the maximum amount of time, money and emotion into planning your move and sees this as an excellent negotiating opportunity.

It is hard to know what to advise if this happens to you. Your natural reaction will be to tell your vendor to get stuffed but, in a buoyant market, it may prove impossible to buy a similar house for the same price. In addition to any financial loss you need to take account of the emotional cost and inconvenience that would be caused if you have to start all over again. I hate to say it but there are certain circumstances where the best thing to do is to swallow your pride and pay the extra money.

EXCHANGE OF CONTRACTS

These days contracts are usually exchanged over the telephone and most solicitors will telephone immediately to let you know the good news. It's safe to open the champagne now. Things can go wrong between exchange and completion but it is extremely rare. I have dealt personally with only three cases.

In the first one the purchasers decided to end their marriage a few days before completion was due to take place. Neither party wanted the house and they ended up forfeiting their 10% deposit. In the second case, the purchaser's father-in-law refused to honour a promise he had made to lend money to fund the purchase after a family row. Again the 10% deposit was forfeited. In the third case, the vendor went bankrupt between exchange of contracts and completion.

Nevertheless there are a number of legal procedures that must be dealt with before completion can take place. The main ones are:

Evidence of title

The vendor's solicitor will send your solicitor a copy of the Deeds or a summary of their content. If your solicitor has any questions he will make 'requisitions on title', i.e. put them in writing.

Draft transfer/conveyance

The vendor's solicitor will send your solicitor a draft transfer (for registered property) or conveyance (for unregistered property). This is the deed which passes the vendor's interest in the property to you.

Mortgages

Your solicitor will write to your mortgage lender to ensure that the mortgage money is available in time for completion.

Engrossment of transfer or conveyance

When both solicitors are satisfied with the terms of the deed it will be 'engrossed', i.e. a final version will be prepared for signature by both sides.

Signing of final documents

You will be asked to sign the final documents and provide a bankers draft for any further money required to fund completion over and above your mortgage advance.

Final searches

Your solicitor will conduct a bankruptcy search in case the vendor has just been declared bankrupt (in which case the property would no longer be his to sell). He also conducts a Land Charges Search to ensure that no last minute charges have been registered against the property.

These could affect the mortgage lender's security.

THINGS YOU MUST DO BEFORE COMPLETION DAY

Choose a removal firm

All removal firms are not the same. The cost of making the wrong choice could be the loss of furnishings and ornaments that have taken a lifetime to collect. The best way to choose a removal firm is by personal recommendation. Ask your estate agent, friends and colleagues if they can recommend a good one. Always get more than one quotation and be sure to base the final decision on reputation as well as on price.

Removals only versus full packing service
Most removal firms offer a variety of service levels, ranging from a full packing service where they will literally do everything, to a basic service where they provide only the lorry and a single working driver. You will need to think carefully about the service that you need and be sure that the quotations that you get from different firms are all for the same level of service.

Insurance
Many otherwise reputable removal firms limit their maximum liability for loss or damage to an absurdly low amount, sometimes just a few pounds per item. There are two ways to get round this problem. The first is to arrange for the necessary additional cover through your own household insurer. The second is to find another removal firm.

Perhaps if more people did the latter the removals industry would be forced to start making proper arrangements for the protection of its customers.

Moving yourself
Moving yourself is hard work and it may not save you as much money as you think. Once you add up the cost of van hire and the hire of the chests or specialist removal cartons (without which things will get broken) you may well decide that the saving is not worth it.

If you do decide to go it alone, these tips will help things to go smoothly.

◆ Van hire – go to a large specialist depot. Many do an all-in removals package which includes van, carton and trolley hire. Remember that they will need to see your driving licence on the day of hiring.

◆ Van size – if in doubt get the larger one. A larger van will allow more careful packing and reduce breakages.

◆ Allow plenty of time – it will always take you longer than you think to move house so start early.

◆ Anticipate making more than one journey. The contents of an average three-bedroom house often do not fit into a 7.5 ton box van (which is the largest that you can hire without an HGV licence). Allow time for a second or third journey.

Arrange the utilities

Arrangements for the new house
Unless you want to move into your new home by

torchlight, arrangements must be made well in advance.

Gas/electricity/water

Phone the new gas, electricity and water companies. Tell them that you are taking over the supply and that you do not want the service to be discontinued. Ask for written confirmation. Be sure to read the meters as soon as you arrive at the new property.

Telephone

If your new property has the same exchange code, you will have the option of keeping your old phone number. If not you will usually be given a choice between taking over your vendor's old number or having a new one. Make sure of your arrangements well in advance and ask for written confirmation.

Arrangements for the old house

Be sure to contact all the utilities to inform them that you are moving. Ask for a final account to be sent to your new address. Don't forget to read the meters before you go.

Mail

The Post Office offers an excellent mail-forwarding service at a very reasonable cost. It is well worth purchasing this service for at least a year in order to ensure that important post doesn't go astray.

COMPLETION DAY

Such is the perversity of the home-buying process that things can go wrong even on completion day itself. Although such problems are fairly rare, it is important to keep in touch with your solicitor throughout the day. Two specific problems are worth mentioning:

Delay in receiving the money

The money to fund the purchase of each property in the chain will almost certainly be sent by telegraphic transfer. In this age of satellite communications you might think that money could be transferred between banks instantly. You would be wrong. The system is terribly inefficient. It often takes several hours for funds to be transferred. What is more there is a shut-off time (usually 1.00 p.m.) after which any funds sent will probably not arrive until the next day.

Due to the inadequacies of the system, the non-arrival of the completion monies is a fairly common problem. If you do not receive the money for your sale you will not be able to complete on your purchase, indeed completion for the whole chain could be delayed until the next day. The inconvenience, cost and legal implications of this delay can be horrendous. Every purchaser in the chain will be contractually obliged to complete by a certain time of day (usually 1.00 p.m.). Should they not do so they will be legally liable for any extra expenses incurred by their vendor. The result can be a lawyer's field day with everyone blaming everyone else for the delay.

Unfortunately there is not much that you can do to avoid this problem although it is worth phoning your solicitor at around 12.00 midday to check that everything is OK. If there is a problem you will have at least an hour to solve it.

Arguments over the release of keys

Until the vendor has received the completion money he will not release the keys to you. This can be extremely frustrating; your removal men are waiting about doing nothing. Unfortunately there is very little that you can do about it. You can try asking the vendor to release the keys but, in view of the awful consequences that could ensue in the event that you moved into the property and were then unable to pay for it, he is very unlikely to agree to do so. If you are not able to complete on completion day you may be able to claim compensation for any additional costs that you incur from your own purchaser or from your mortgage lender if they were responsible for causing the delay.

ARRIVING AT YOUR NEW HOUSE

Congratulations. You have done it – but before you completely relax it is worth doing three last things.

Test the services

Check immediately that you have gas, electricity, water and a telephone. If any of these services have been disconnected you will need to get on to the suppliers immediately.

Read the meters

It is all too easy to get caught for the previous owner's bill. Check the meters and make a careful note of the readings as soon as you move in.

Check the fixtures and fittings list

Check to make sure that all fixtures and fittings have been left that should have been. If something major has been taken in defiance of the contracted agreement you can threaten to sue for its return.

Part Two
Selling Your House

Introduction

A great many 'how to sell your house' books have been published during recent years. Some cover the financial aspects of a move such as raising a mortgage; some cover the legal side of the transaction and some cover how to sell without using an estate agent. However, during the whole of the time that I have been associated with the property market I have never come across a book that explained how to choose and get the best out of an estate agent.

This struck me as very strange. Most house sellers sell through an estate agent and yet there was no such thing as a consumer's guide to estate agency. I felt that there should be, so in this section of the book I have set out to answer some of the many questions that I have been asked as a consultant during the last 15 years.

This section is in three parts. Chapters 14–16 cover how to establish a property's value and choose the right estate agent. Ideally this section should be read about eight weeks before the property is put onto the market. Chapters 17–20 explain how a good agent should go about finding a buyer. This section should be read as soon as the property is put onto the market. The final chapters explain some of the common sales problems and give advice on how to overcome them. This section should be used as a reference section to dip into as and when problems occur.

(14)

Establishing What Your Property is Worth

DOING YOUR OWN RESEARCH

Before you invite an estate agent to value your property you must first establish what it is worth. This may seem like a contradiction in terms but the fact is that estate agents' valuations are often inaccurate. This can happen for a number of reasons:

1. **Deliberate over-valuation** – some estate agents give deliberately over-optimistic valuations because they know that it will help them to get more properties onto their books.

2. **Poor research** – an estate agent should have up-to-date knowledge about the prices achieved for other properties in the area which have recently sold. Poor research is a very common reason for an inaccurate valuation.

3. **Inexperience** – too many firms of estate agents send staff out on valuation appointments who do not have sufficient experience to value accurately.

4. **Poor local knowledge** – even an experienced estate agent will not be able to value a property accurately until he has been working in the local area for several months.

The only way to protect yourself against the consequences of an inaccurate valuation is to undertake comprehensive price research on your own behalf. In some countries the actual selling price achieved in every property transaction is a matter of public record. In the UK this information is often not publicly available and a degree of subterfuge may be required to obtain the necessary background information.

If you have not already done so, you should reconsider the idea of registering with some of the local agents as a buyer in order to obtain a selection of sales particulars of properties that are similar to your own. If you really do not wish to undertake this type of research, an alternative would be to look through back issues of the local property newspaper to find similar properties (back issues of the local papers are available from the library). The more properties you can find, the more likely it is that your personal valuation will be accurate.

USING THE INFORMATION

The value of a property is determined by two factors: the prices achieved for similar properties that have recently been sold, and the asking prices of properties that are currently on the market and are competing for the same buyers as your own.

It is relatively easy to establish the value of a house in a road when there are other similar properties. The typical process would be:

Step 1   Research the asking prices of the last five or six properties in the road that have been offered for sale.

Step 2   Ignore properties which were markedly cheaper or more expensive than the others (there is always a reason).

Step 3   Average the price of the remaining properties.

Step 4   Deduct 5% from the final price to allow for the average difference between the asking and selling prices.

VALUING A MORE INDIVIDUAL PROPERTY

If you own a more individual property you will need to apply a number of adjustment factors to the comparable properties that are available. Some of the most important factors to take into account are:

Extensions and improvements

You will not generally recover the full cost of extensions and improvements. The proportion of the original cost that is recovered will depend upon the nature of the improvement, for example:

High cost recovery (up to 100%)
◆ Addition of extra bedroom in a style that is in keeping with the original property.
◆ Addition of central heating.
◆ Redecoration in a neutral style.
◆ Addition of a garage.

Medium cost recovery (up to 50%)

♦ Addition of ground-floor flat-roofed extension.
♦ Addition of conservatory.
♦ Fitted kitchen.
♦ Modernisation of bathroom.
♦ Loft conversion.

Low cost recovery (less than 25%)

♦ Addition of outdoor swimming pool.
♦ Addition of ground-floor bathroom.
♦ Double glazing.
♦ Cavity wall insulation.

Negative improvements

Some improvements can substantially reduce the value of the property, for example:

♦ Extensions that occupy the entire garden.
♦ Stone cladding.
♦ Double glazing on period property.
♦ Removal of period features (fireplaces, decorative plasterwork, etc.)

Repairs

As with improvements, you are unlikely to recover the full cost of repairs that have been made to a property. Most buyers underestimate the cost of repairs and some are prepared to pay a premium for a house in poor condition in order to have the satisfaction of refurbishing it in their own taste.

Area

In many towns a house in one road can command a very substantial premium over houses in the next. It is impossible to generalise about this but the boundaries are usually well-known locally.

Location

A house on a busy road or one backing onto a railway line will be worth substantially less than an identical house in a quiet street nearby. An extremely adverse location could reduce the value of a property by up to half.

New developments

Many people will pay a premium to live in a brand new house. All new properties must therefore be excluded from your comparable evidence.

CHECKING THE ACCURACY OF YOUR VALUATION

You can check the accuracy of your personal valuation by cross-referencing it in a number of ways:

How much did you pay?

Local estate agents will be able to provide you with a table showing the average rise in property values for each year since you purchased your property. Alternatively you can look on the Land Registry, *www.landreg.gov.uk*. Add the appropriate percentage increase to the price which you originally paid for your property. How does it compare to your own valuation?

Current value of properties which you rejected as a purchaser

Before you bought your present property, you will almost certainly have viewed and rejected a number of alternative properties. Check to see if any of these properties, or others that are similar to them, are currently on the market. How does the asking price of each of these properties compare to your own valuation?

Remortgage valuations
If you have remortgaged your house at any time, try adding the average percentage rise in property values since the remortgage to the surveyor's valuation. How does this figure compare to your own valuation?

Friends and acquaintances who have recently bought and sold
People are strangely reticent about revealing the price that they paid or obtained for their property but there is no harm in asking. People often tell their neighbours that they paid more or less for their property than they really did. You should therefore treat all information obtained in this way with the greatest suspicion, particularly information which is passed on by a third party.

Internet research
Look on the Internet to find details of houses like yours that are currently on the market.

Once you have done everything possible to research and check the accuracy of your personal valuation you are ready to begin to prepare for the estate agents' valuation appointments.

PREPARING YOUR PROPERTY FOR SALE

Presentation is vital
The maxim 'presentation is vital' was never more true

than when selling a house. It is therefore extremely important to carry out any necessary cosmetic work before you put your property on the market.

House buyers form their impressions very quickly – indeed research shows that half of all buyers make the final decision before they even get inside the front door! If such a high proportion of buyers are going to make their decision from outside then this is where you too must start.

Go and stand in the street at least 100 yards away from your property. Take a good hard look and try to see it through the eyes of someone who has never seen it before. What do you see? Have the neighbours' houses been decorated more recently than yours? If so consider redecorating at least the front elevation.

Move slowly forwards, ten yards at a time. What do you see as you move closer? Could your teenage son be persuaded to park his battered old car somewhere else for a few weeks? Are any tiles missing from the roof? Does the hedge need trimming? Is the front fence in good condition? Does the front garden need tidying?

Enter the front garden. Does the gate operate smoothly? Is the front door in good decorative condition? Are there cobwebs in the porch? Does the door bell work?

Open the front door and step inside. Take a long critical look at the entrance hall. Bear in mind that it is the first room that potential purchasers will see and consider whether any work is necessary to brighten it up. Before you leave the entrance hall think carefully about what order the rooms in the house should be shown in. It is important to ensure that buyers see the most attractive rooms first.

Go round the house in the order that purchasers will see it and check each room thoroughly. In particular look for the following:

- Does any room need redecorating?
- Are there any stains or damp patches?
- Are there any cracks?
- Do the carpets need cleaning?
- Do any light bulbs need replacing?
- Are any windows overshadowed by trees or foliage?
- Are the windows dirty?
- Is the garden tidy?
- Are the fences in good order?

Decorating to sell

If any room does need redecorating it is best to stick to light neutral colours which will make the room look bigger and lighter. Save expressing your individualism for your next house.

More extensive works

Generally speaking it is not worth undertaking more major works in order to facilitate a sale. If you are thinking of undertaking repair work, you should bear in mind that most purchasers tend to underestimate the true cost of repairs so you are likely to be better off by leaving them as they are. If you are thinking of undertaking cosmetic work you should bear in mind that most buyers would prefer to buy a cheaper property and install their own choice of kitchen, bathroom or carpets, etc.

Finishing touches
In addition to the above you might also consider:

1. **Net curtains** – net curtains block out a great deal of natural light and can also make rooms look smaller. Consider taking them down whilst the house is on the market.

2. **Curtains** – rooms can be made to seem very dark by heavy curtains which cannot be drawn back off the windows. Consider tying such curtains back whilst the house is on the market.

3. **Furniture** – large pieces of furniture will make rooms seem smaller. Consider repositioning or even storing such items whilst the house is on the market.

4. **Flowers** – a hanging basket in the porch or fresh flowers in the entrance hall can make a real difference to a buyer's first impression of your house.

When considering all of the above, bear in mind the golden rule that 'the sooner they see it the more important it is'. A dingy entrance hall could be extremely off-putting; your daughter's fluorescent purple fourth bedroom will have less effect on a potential purchaser's decision.

Organise a trial viewing

Once you have attended to all the necessary jobs, ask a friend to 'view' your property. Ask them to point out anything that you have missed. Ask them also for their honest opinion on one very important matter. How does your house smell? I am not joking. Despite the fact that smell is one of our most powerful senses, many people do not realise that the human nose is only programmed to detect new smells. To you Fido stopped 'smelling' when he was a 12-week-old puppy. To strangers he could now smell strongly enough to prevent a sale for months! Even the bravest estate agent will not tell you this – find a friend who will.

Consider paying for a surveyor's report

Very few people consider instructing a surveyor to look at a house that they are selling, but a survey report can be a valuable marketing tool. Many buyers are nervous about making an offer for a house for fear that problems will later be revealed on survey. If this does happen, the cost to them could be several hundred pounds in abortive legal and survey fees and two to three weeks' wasted time.

A survey report is not transferable and a buyer would have no legal comeback on the surveyor if the report were later found to be inaccurate. However, the availability of a survey report can do a great deal to allay a buyer's fears and it could prove to be well worth its cost. A survey report is particularly valuable if you are selling a house that is large, old or in poor condition.

Case study

John and Sarah S asked three agents to value their property, a traditional three-bedroom semi in a road of 100 similar houses. Agent 'A' valued it at £70,000, Agent 'B' at £72,000 and Agent 'C' at £80,000. John and Sarah instructed Agent 'C' at an asking price of £79,950 and signed a 20-week sole agency contract.

After four weeks no one had viewed the property so John rang the agent to ask why. The agent said that he thought that the price was too high and advised a reduction. When John reminded the agent that he had said it was worth £80,000 the agent replied 'Valuation is not an exact science, a property is only worth what someone is prepared to pay for it.'

John said that if that was the case he would withdraw his property and give it to Agent 'A' whose original valuation had been more accurate. The agent replied that if he did this he would sue John and Sarah for breaking their 20-week sole agency contract. Faced with no other alternative John and Sarah reduced the asking price of their property and Agent 'C' sold it shortly afterwards for £70,000.

With hindsight John and Sarah wished that they had instructed Agents 'A' or 'B'.

(15)

Choosing An Estate Agent

DECIDING WHETHER YOU NEED AN ESTATE AGENT

More than three-quarters of all house sellers use an estate
agent. They do so because they believe that, even after
allowing for commission, an agent will achieve a higher
price for their property than they could achieve themselves. They are usually right.

Why will an estate agent achieve a higher price?

The price that is achieved for a property is largely
determined by the law of supply and demand. If a
property is exposed to a greater number of potential
buyers, it will usually sell for a higher price.

One of the most important functions of an estate agent is,
therefore, to act as an efficient net to catch every potential
house buyer in the price range. When it comes to finding
potential buyers, an estate agent has five important
advantages over the private seller. They are:

1. **Newspaper advertising** – an estate agent will run
   prominent advertisements in the local newspapers
   each week. The number of enquiries generated is
   related very closely to the size of the advertisement. A
   small private advertisement would do well to generate
   half a dozen enquiries. The estate agent's full-page
   advertisement will generate many times this number.

A second point to consider regarding advertising is that many potential purchasers, particularly those from out of the area, buy a local newspaper only once. Having registered with all the local agents, they then wait to be contacted with details of suitable properties. By advertising for only one week the private vendor will reach only a fraction of these buyers.

2. **Internet presence** – most estate agents advertise on at least one of the major portals. These receive thousands of hits a day from prospective buyers.

3. **High street premises** – many buyers like to register by calling into the estate agent's office in person. Out-of-town buyers in particular tend to find 'estate agents' row' and register with all the agents in it. The lack of high street premises will further reduce the number of potential purchasers that the private vendor is able to attract.

4. *Yellow Pages* – many buyers register with agents by working through *Yellow Pages*. The lack of an entry here will further hamper the private vendor.

5. **'For Sale' boards** – the typical estate agent will have several dozen 'For Sale' boards up at any one time. Each one of these boards will attract several new buyers and cumulatively they will be responsible for attracting around a quarter of all buyers. The private vendor with just his own single 'For Sale' will fail to attract most of these purchasers.

Given all these advantages, an estate agent should be able to attract many times more purchasers for a property than a private vendor. Consequently, even a bad agent will usually be able to achieve a better price for your property than you could yourself.

Other benefits of using an agent

In addition to finding the maximum number of potential purchasers, a good estate agent will be able to help with your sale in several other important ways. These include:

1. **Valuation advice** – a good agent will give advice on the value of your property and help you to decide on the optimum asking price.

2. **Marketing** – a good agent will play an active role in persuading potential purchasers to view your property.

3. **Security** – a good agent will check out potential viewers to ensure that they are genuine.

4. **Negotiation** – a good agent will use his negotiation skills to obtain the highest possible price.

5. **Qualification** – a good agent will check out your prospective buyers to ensure that they are actually in a position to proceed with the transaction.

6. **Supervision** – a good agent will keep a close eye on your sale and help to resolve any problems that arise prior to completion.

It is certainly possible to sell a house privately but there is no doubt that a good agent will earn his fee many times over. I would urge you to use one.

FINDING THE RIGHT ESTATE AGENT

In most large towns there is a bewildering selection of estate agents to choose from. To the casual observer they might appear to be all very much the same. On closer examination you will find that they most certainly are not. The best agent in the town might be able to achieve thousands of pounds more for your property than his least effective competitor. With this sort of money at stake it is worth going to considerable trouble to choose the right agent for the job.

The telltale signs that differentiate an outstanding agent from an average one can be grouped under two categories: the 'marketing campaign' and the 'service standards'.

THE MARKETING CAMPAIGN

The number of potential purchasers that each agent has on his books will be governed by the effectiveness of his marketing campaign. The most effective agent could have three or four times more buyers on his register than his least effective competitor and this gives him a much better chance of achieving a premium price for your property. The effectiveness of each agent's marketing campaign can be judged by looking at the three key areas of advertising, board presence and office position.

Newspaper advertising

Newspaper advertising is the single most important source of potential purchasers and it is, therefore, worth taking some trouble to assess each agent's effectiveness in this area. Collect together all the local newspapers for a three to four week period and look for the following features:

1. **Size** – the leading agents will nearly always have the largest advertisements. There is a direct correlation between the size of the advertisement and the number of enquiries generated.

2. **Choice of publication** – advertising costs vary widely between different newspapers and, generally speaking, advertisers get what they pay for. If in doubt you might consider phoning the local newspapers to enquire about advertising rates and circulation figures so that you can make your own assessment of which agent has the highest local advertising budget.

3. **Position** – certain pages in a newspaper generate far more enquiries than others. Generally speaking:
   - the nearer the front the better
   - right-hand pages are better than left-hand pages
   - the front cover, back cover and centre pages usually get a good response.

   The leading agents usually book the prime positions on a long-term contract. You should be cautious about using an agent who has a consistently poor position.

4. **Frequency** – the leading agents will advertise every week throughout the year (with the possible exception of December). You should be cautious about using an agent who advertises only sporadically.

5. **Layout** – the advertisement should be easy to read with an attractive layout and plenty of space between the properties. Advertisements that cram too many properties into a small space generate fewer enquiries.

6. **Colour** – full-colour advertisements generate far more enquiries than black-and-white ones. If only two or three agents are advertising in colour, they will have a considerable advantage over their competitors.

7. **Variety** – beware of the agent who advertises the same houses every week. He may be having trouble attracting new instructions (and there is usually a reason for this).

8. **Content** – what sort of properties are advertised by each agent? Are they cheaper or more expensive than your own? There is no point putting an ordinary house with an up-market agent or vice versa.

Website

Check out each agent's website. Try searching for a specific property. Is it easy to use? Is it up to date? Would-be buyers will be turned off by an ineffective website.

Board presence

Estate agents' boards are another very important source of enquiries. Do a rough count of which agents have the largest number of boards up in your area. It is likely that each of these boards will have already generated several enquiries from potential purchasers for your property. Pay particular attention to 'Sold' boards. The agent who has recently sold several houses in your road could well be the best agent to handle the sale of your house.

Office position

A large percentage of potential purchasers like to register their requirements in person. The position and prominence of an estate agent's office is often, therefore, an important factor. The prominent high street office will usually register several times as many potential purchasers as its small backstreet competitor.

STANDARDS OF CUSTOMER SERVICE

Before you rush off to instruct the agent with the biggest advertisement and the most prominent office, you should pause to consider that registering the largest number of potential purchasers is not an automatic guarantee of success. In order to sell houses effectively, an agent needs to persuade potential purchasers to view the properties that they have for sale. It is here that so many agents fall down.

There is only one way to establish which of the local agents offers the best standard of service and that is to register with them all as a buyer. If you are moving locally you can register as a genuine purchaser. If you are not buying locally you could register as a purchaser for a property that is similar to the one which you wish to sell, perhaps saying that your present property is rented. You will find that the level of service which you receive as a purchaser varies enormously between agents. The signs of an effective agent are:

1. **Initial response** – the telephone should be answered promptly and cheerfully.

2. **Rapport** – the agent should work hard to build a rapport rather than just reading questions off a list.

3. **Qualification** – the agent should establish quickly whether you are in a position to buy immediately or

whether you have a property yet to sell. This will enable him to work more effectively by spending more time with his best prospects.

4. **Sales effort** – the agent should describe a couple of suitable properties over the phone and ask you for an immediate commitment to view them. This is far more effective than just passively sending out details.

5. **Property details** – an accurately chosen selection of property details should arrive by post the next working day. Some firms might even deliver details by hand to local purchasers. The details should be attractively presented, preferably with full colour photographs.

6. **Telephone follow-up** – the effective agent will telephone you approximately 24 hours after you have received the details and make another attempt to get a viewing appointment. Purchasers who are followed up by telephone are far more likely to view than those who are left to contact the agent themselves.

7. **Ongoing follow-up** – the effective agent will continue to telephone you at least once a week to try to persuade you to view properties that are new to the market.

8. **Persistence** – to be effective an agent must be persistent. You need someone who will really *sell* your property, not just wait for someone to buy it. However, the effective agent should know when to give up gracefully and should never become over-aggressive.

You will usually find that the service given by one or two agents stands head and shoulders above the service given by the rest. These agents should definitely be included on your shortlist.

Owning up

It is unlikely that you will ever need to own up to your subterfuge. You can tell the agents that did not measure up that you have now found a property to buy. The agents that you do choose to invite to value your property will often not notice that someone on their applicant register has asked for a valuation appointment. If they do, you can simply admit that you wanted to test their service before instructing them. They will probably be quite flattered to have been chosen by such an objective process.

HOW NOT TO CHOOSE AN ESTATE AGENT

As a home owner you are likely to receive regular approaches from agents who are touting for business. These will come in a number of formats:

1. **The printed leaflet** – a typical message would be 'Now is the time to sell. Call Bloggs estate agents for a free valuation without obligation.' Many estate agents deliver tens of thousands of such leaflets every year. The fact that you have received one does not mean that the company who sent it will be any better able to sell your house than the others.

2. **The photocopied letter** – a typical message would be 'Dear Householder, We have just sold a house in your road and urgently need similar properties in the area.' This type of letter deserves to be taken a little more seriously. The agent would not have chosen your road if he did not have a demand for houses in it. However,

if you do respond to such an approach you should ask for the agent to prove that he really has sold a property and that he has other buyers available for similar properties in the area.

3. **The individually addressed letter** – The format of this letter will be similar to the photocopied letter described above and it should be dealt with in a similar way. The fact that it is addressed to you by name means only that the agent has looked up your name on the electoral register, which is available in the public library.

Although it may sometimes be worth responding to a touting letter, you should not allow the receipt of one to unduly influence your choice of agent. You are far more likely to find the right agent to market your property by objective research than by responding to a cleverly written letter.

SELECTING THE FINAL SHORTLIST

Having finished your study of all the local agents you will be in a position to compile a shortlist of agents that you wish to see. Sometimes one agent will win hands down in every category, but more often than not you will be forced to compromise. Perhaps the agent with the biggest advertisement and the most prominent office gave you very poor services as a buyer. This could be a business that is in decline. Perhaps the dynamic manager who built the office up has recently been replaced by someone of a lower calibre. Whatever the reason, such a company is best avoided. At the other end of the scale you may have received outstanding service from an agent with a backstreet office and sporadic advertising. Again you should be cautious. Service is important but it cannot make up for a lack of potential buyers to sell to.

The safest choice would be to confine your list to companies who score reasonably well in both the key areas of effective marketing and effective customer service. On this basis you should select three or four agents to value your property.

ARRANGING THE VALUATION APPOINTMENT

When you telephone to arrange a valuation appointment, the agent will want to ask you a number of questions. Beware. It is probably not in your best interest to answer them all at this time. The likely questions can be divided into three categories:

Questions about the property

The agent will ask for a detailed description of your property. He needs this information in order to research its value prior to his visit. You should describe your property accurately and thoroughly, paying particular attention to any unusual features such as an extension.

Questions about you

The agent will also ask for a lot of background information about you. He will want to know the reason for your move, your anticipated timescale and whether you have already contacted other agents. The agent's purpose in asking such questions is to ascertain whether you are serious about moving or whether you just want a valuation. Your answers to these questions will determine how seriously your enquiry is taken and also, very often, the seniority of the member of staff sent out to see you. For this reason these questions must be answered with some care. In particular:

- Never admit to being in a hurry to sell. This could mean a lower valuation.

- Always say that you will be inviting several agents around before deciding who to instruct on a sole agency basis (a more senior member of staff will often be sent to sell the firm's service against competition).

Questions about the property's value

Some agents will ask you what price you are hoping to achieve for your property over the telephone. If you reveal this there is a real danger that the agent will tell you the price that you want to hear instead of giving you a properly researched valuation. You should therefore decline to answer this question at this time. Say something like 'I do have a price in mind but I should like to hear your opinion first.'

Having answered the agent's questions, the next thing to do is to agree on a time for the appointment. Your valuation appointment is an extremely important occasion, and it is my belief that it is an occasion where two heads are better than one. If you have a partner, then both of you should be present. If not you might consider asking a trusted friend to sit through each appointment with you.

The amount of time each agent will wish to spend with you will vary widely but, to be on the safe side 1 ½ hours should be allowed between appointments. It is embarras-

sing for everyone if the next agent arrives before the
previous one has left. The best time for an appointment is
undoubtedly a weekday when most agents will have more
time to explain their service fully. On no account should
an agent be invited to undertake a valuation after dark.
Artificial light makes a property look so different that
accurate valuation is impossible.

Finally, do not be frightened to stand firm on your
preferred appointment times. Agents often try to sound
busier than they are in order to impress potential clients
and may be able to move 'another appointment' if you
insist on a particular time.

MEETING YOUR ESTATE AGENT

Background and first impressions

Estate agency is a profession that is full of eccentrics. It is
therefore important to resist the temptation to judge each
agent on the basis of first impressions alone. The
dishevelled-looking chap who arrives by bicycle, ten
minutes late for the appointment, could very easily be
the best agent for the job.

After exchanging pleasantries, the agent will probably
wish to start the appointment by sitting down with you to
discuss the background to your move. During this part of
the appointment the agent will be trying to establish three
things:

◆ How serious are you about moving?
◆ What is your timescale?
◆ Why are you moving?

The experienced estate agent will make this stage of the appointment seem like nothing more than an informal exchange of pleasantries but in fact every single question will have a purpose. For example the purpose of a question like 'are you moving with work?' might be to find out if your company will be paying the fees so that a higher than usual commission rate may be quoted. Your answers to all such questions should reassure the agent that you are serious about moving. However, you must at the same time be very careful not to say anything that may later prejudice your negotiating position. If, for example, you are desperate to sell your property quickly, you should keep this to yourself, at very least until an asking price and a commission level have been agreed and preferably until the property has been on the market for a couple of weeks. If you do not, you may find that you are quoted a lower asking price, an increased commission level, or both!

Having established the background to your move, the agent will next wish to look round the property. I would recommend that he should be allowed to do so alone. During this initial inspection tour the agent will value your property by comparing it with all the others that he has seen. This process requires great concentration and the valuation will probably be more accurate if the agent is not obliged to make small talk during his inspection.

On his return the agent should be ready to discuss his valuation with you. I say should because just occasionally you will come across an agent who is unwilling to discuss his valuation without first discussing it with his colleagues back at the office. If the property is very large or unusual then there is some justification for this. If it is not you should ask the agent bluntly why he feels unable to give you a valuation on the spot. The most likely reasons are inexperience or lack of preparation. If you suspect that either is the case you should find another agent.

AGREEING AN ASKING PRICE

Beware of the agent who overvalues

The worst possible way to choose an estate agent is to instruct the one that quotes the highest asking price. Unfortunately this is exactly how many home owners make their decision. A minority of estate agents exploit this by deliberately over-valuing the properties that they see in order to get instructions. Once instructed, they will try to persuade the client to reduce the asking price in the hope that the property can still be sold before the end of the sole agency period. Such agents should be avoided like the plague. Fortunately they are very easy to spot.

An agent who deliberately overvalues will spend the whole valuation appointment trying to find out the price that you want to hear. The least subtle will ask you directly for the price that you are hoping to achieve. Most will try to find out by more subtle methods.

One common method is to ask you how long you have owned the house and how much you originally paid for it. By applying the appropriate annual adjustment factors the agent will be able to calculate the likely present value. An alternative method is to ask how much you are intending to spend on your next house and then later on by how much you are planning to increase your present mortgage. Some very simple mathematics will give the agent the price that you are hoping to achieve for your present house. A more subtle technique involves the agent mentioning the prices of a number of other houses that have been sold recently. Each time a price is mentioned the agent will watch closely for your reaction. Each time you look disappointed, he will raise his 'valuation' for your property until he is sure that you will be happy with the figure that he gives you.

You have absolutely nothing to gain from revealing your assessment of the property's value before you have heard the agent's opinion and my advice would be to respond to all such questions by saying something like 'I really would like to hear your valuation before I discuss my expectations with you.' Faced with this response the agent will have no choice but to give his own opinion of value.

Control your reaction

However disappointed you are by the agent's figure, it is important not to show it at this stage. In order to obtain the maximum benefit from the agent's experience, you must first work calmly through four further stages:

Stage 1 – Confirmation

Some agents try to leave themselves room for manoeuvre by saying that the property is worth between £50–£55,000. It is important to try to pin the agent down to a precise figure. Try asking him in what circumstances he would expect to achieve both the lower and the higher figure.

Stage 2 – Qualification

The main purpose of this stage is to prevent an agent from trying to wriggle out of his original valuation when challenged. He may try to do this using words such as:

♦ My original figure of £65,000 is the price I expect to obtain after negotiation. The asking price of course would be much higher.

To avoid this you should ask the agent to confirm every aspect of his valuation by asking questions such as:

♦ What would be your recommended asking price?
♦ What price would you expect to obtain after negotiation?
♦ How long would you expect it to take to find a buyer at this price?

Stage 3 – Justification

Ask the agent to explain to you the exact process by which he arrived at his valuation. In particular ask him which comparable properties he took into account before arriving at his final figure. A good agent should be able to justify his valuation without hesitation, by referring to at least three comparable properties. A really good agent will have brought the sales particulars of all comparable properties with him to the appointment.

Stage 4 – Negotiation

Once you have heard both the agent's valuation and his justification for it, you can safely reveal your own expectation and the process by which you arrived at it. The process of negotiation which is likely to follow is probably best demonstrated by the use of some fictitious case studies.

Example A: undervaluation – vendor concedes
Agent's initial valuation £90,000: recommended asking price £93,950.

Vendor   I'm sorry to tell you that your valuation is £5,000 less than I was hoping to achieve and I'd like to tell you how I arrived at my figure. I have two justifications:

1. The property opposite which is identical to mine was sold eight weeks ago for £96,000.
2. I believe that number 86, which has no garage, was also sold last month for £89,000.

On this evidence I really do expect to get £95,000 for mine.

Agent   The original price agreed for the house opposite was indeed £96,000 but the building society valuer down-valued it on survey to £90,000 and that is what it sold for. I therefore stand by my valuation of £90,000.

Vendor   But number 89 sold for £89,950 and it doesn't have a garage.

Agent   When number 89 was sold the house opposite was for sale at £99,950. This made number 86 seem good value. Now that it is known that the house opposite sold for £90,000 this sets a ceiling on the price achievable in the road.

Vendor	I accept your argument but I would like to quote an initial asking price of £96,950 not £93,950.
Agent	I believe that the price would discourage potential viewers.
Vendor	All right, then £95,950.
Agent	I will try it at that figure for 14 days but we must review the price after that.

Example B: undervaluation – agent concedes
Agent's initial valuation £65,000; recommended asking price £66,950.

Vendor	I am disappointed by your figure. Number 12 sold at £69,000 and number 19 is for sale at £69,950.
Agent	We sold a house in the next road a few weeks ago for £65,000. I believe my valuation is correct.
Vendor	You didn't refer to number 12 or to number 19 when citing your comparable evidence. I have to ask whether you took them into account in your valuation.
Agent	We didn't handle those sales.
Vendor	That doesn't answer my question.
Agent	I have based my valuation on the house which we sold in the next road.
Vendor	In view of the price achieved for number 12, I should like to quote £69,950 for my property.

	Would you be prepared to take it on at that figure?
Agent	Yes.
Vendor	Very well. If I instruct you it will be at £69,950.

Example C: overvaluation – agent concedes
Agent's initial valuation £45,000; recommended asking price £46,750.

Vendor	My own valuation was £3,000 less than yours. I based it on two other identical flats in the block, numbers 4 and 22, both of which have sold for £42,000 within the last three months. Could you explain to me again how you arrived at your figure?
Agent	The even-numbered flats are at the front of the block. They always seem to sell for less.
Vendor	That wasn't true when I bought this flat. What has changed since?
Agent	I don't know, but it is generally true.
Vendor	When did you last sell a flat in this block?
Agent	I've been in the agency for five years. The company must have sold loads.
Vendor	How about you personally?
Agent	Well, I only moved to this branch a couple of months ago.
Vendor	Whilst I would like to get £45,000 I don't believe that I can do it in the time available. If

I instruct you it will be at a lower figure, but thank you for your advice.

The final decision

Always remember that the final decision on an asking price is yours and yours alone. There is absolutely nothing to stop you instructing an agent at an asking price that is different from the one recommended. The agent's job is to advise, your job is to weigh up advice from as many different sources as possible and to decide. No one else should make that decision for you.

ASSESSING THE AGENT'S SALES PRESENTATION

Giving an accurate valuation is one thing, achieving that price is quite another. Your decision as to which agent to instruct cannot therefore be made on the basis of the valuation alone.

Once an asking price has been agreed, the estate agent should, of his own accord, tell you more about the service that his company offers. It is best to leave the agent to highlight the key features of his service but if necessary you should prompt him in order to ensure that the following areas are covered:

1. Experience
- How long has he personally been in the business?
- How long has he worked in the local area?
- How long has he worked for his present employer?
- How experienced are the other members of his team?

2. Company background
- Who owns the business?
- How long has the firm been established?

3. Advertising
- Where does the firm advertise?
- Do the advertisements have any special features (e.g. colour photographs)?

4. Property particulars
- Does the company use colour photographs on its particulars?

5. Coverage
- Does the company have offices in other local towns?
- If so, will your property details be available there?

6. Opening hours
- What are the usual opening hours?
- Is the office staffed by full-time people at weekends?

7. Sales methods
- Are buyers usually contacted by telephone or by post?
- Will the agent accompany viewings or will you be left to show buyers round yourself?

8. Qualification/security
- How does the agency check to ensure that buyers are genuine?
- How will they check that buyers can afford to buy your property before arranging an appointment?

9. Sales progressing
- What action will the agent take to ensure that your sale reaches a satisfactory conclusion?

10. Recent results
- Has the agent recently sold other properties in your area?
- How many houses do they usually sell each month? (They might not tell you but there is no harm in asking.)

11. Testimonials
- Can the agent show you testimonials from satisfied clients?

By the end of this part of the interview you will probably have a very good idea about whether you wish to instruct the agent or not. The final factor in you decision will be the commission level.

NEGOTIATING THE FEE
The maxim 'you get what you pay for' is true for most things in life and estate agency is no exception. If you are quoted an unexpectedly low fee the first thing to do is to check that you are being quoted for a full estate agency service. You will very often find that the lower fee is in fact being quoted by a property shop or by an agent who operates on an exclusive agency basis.

Property shops versus conventional estate agents
Property shops charge much lower fees than estate agents. They are able to do this because they charge their fee at

the point of instruction and keep it regardless of whether a sale is achieved or not. The inherent disadvantage of paying an up front fee is that the property shop has no financial incentive to sell your house. It is probably because of this that the success rate of most property shops is lower than that of most estate agents. Taking everything into account a conventional estate agent is usually likely to offer better value for money.

Responding to a lower than expected fee
If you are quoted a low fee by a conventional estate agent, you must establish how he is able to undercut his competitors. You might say something like 'The fee that you have quoted is half a percent less than your main competitors. Could I ask how you are able to offer the same service at a lower price?'

On closer examination you will often find that the lower fee is financed by less advertising, fewer staff, cheaper premises or some other such economy. If this is the case you should weigh up very carefully how these economies might affect the agent's ability to achieve the best price for your property.

Responding to a higher than expected fee
If you are quoted a fee that is higher than expected, you should challenge it firmly but politely. You might say something like 'I am impressed by your service but your fee is half a percent more than I've been quoted elsewhere. How can you justify this differential?' Faced with such a challenge the effective agent might try one of two approaches:

(a) He might try to justify the differential by pointing out further features of his service which are not offered by his competitors, e.g. colour advertising or longer opening hours.

(b) He might argue that the same negotiation techniques which enable him to obtain premium fee levels from his clients will also enable him to achieve a premium price for your property!

Both arguments have some merit. It is for you to decide whether you believe that superior marketing or superior negotiation techniques will indeed lead to a higher sale price but my experience is that they often do.

The less effective agent will respond to his fee level being challenged in one of two other ways:

(a) He will immediately match the lower fee. If he does this you must ask whether he would give in so easily when negotiating an offer for your property with a potential purchaser.

(b) He will suggest that the extra commission is added on to your asking price. This is quite indefensible. If the property is really worth more why did the agent not say so sooner? If it is not then you will end up paying his whole fee anyway.

Some non-conventional fee arrangements

Most agents express their fee as a percentage of the selling price but there is no need for the fee to be calculated in this way. The following alternatives may be appropriate in different circumstances. Their introduction may also often help to resolve fee negotiations that have become dead-locked:

The split-percentage fee

Most of an agent's skill is used to persuade a purchaser to increase his offer by the last few thousand pounds. The split-fee arrangement recognises this by giving an agent a much higher reward if he achieves a premium price. A split-fee arrangement works like this:

Conventional fee

Asking price	£109,950
Expected sales price	£100,000
Fee payable £100,000 × 2%	£2,000

Split fee

Asking price	£109,950
Fee agreement	1.5% of the first £95,000 and 10% of any balance achieved above this figure
Price achieved	£105,000
Fee payable	£95,000 × 1.5% = £1,425
+	+ £10,000 × 10% = £1,000
Total fee payable	£2,425

In this example the agent is £425 better off, but the vendor is £4,575 better off!

This sort of arrangement gives the agent a tremendous incentive to achieve a premium price and can be an excellent arrangement for both parties.

The fixed fee

It is agreed that a fee of £X will be paid regardless of what price is achieved for the property. This arrangement would most commonly be used for very expensive properties, or at the agent's instigation, for a very cheap property (e.g. a mobile home) where he wishes to charge a minimum fee but is embarrassed to quote this as 10% of the selling price. Fixed fees have their place but the drawback is that the agent has no financial incentive to achieve a higher price for the vendor.

The part-upfront fee

An agent knows that he will only sell approximately 50% of all the houses that he takes on. The remainder will be withdrawn by vendors who decide not to sell after all or will be sold by another agent. The cost of marketing properties that are not sold is considerable and ultimately this cost has to be recovered from clients who do sell. For this reason agents are often prepared to make a substantial reduction in their commission in return for a relatively small non-refundable advance payment.

For example:

> Usual fee 2% selling price of £100,000 = £2,000
> Alternative £500 advance payment
> 1% fee payable on sale
> Total fee payable £1,500
> Saving to client £500.

This method is only to be recommended if you are absolutely sure that you want to sell your property and if you are also certain about your choice of agent.

The personal bonus

By arrangement with the office manager, you may be able to agree to pay a personal bonus to the individual negotiator who sells your property. This arrangement is particularly appropriate if you need to sell your property quickly. Increasing the agent's commission from 2 to 2.5% would have little effect on the way that the agent marketed your property. Offering a 2% bonus to the individual negotiator who sells the property could do a great deal to ensure that your property is given priority.

I would stress that such arrangements should only be made with the full knowledge and approval of the manager and/or the proprietor. You must also make it clear to the negotiator who receives the bonus that he or she will be responsible for paying income tax on the monies paid.

After considering every possible alternative fee structure and engaging in five or ten minutes of lively negotiation you will be almost ready to make your final choice of agent.

MAKING YOUR FINAL DECISION

At the end of the valuation appointment, the agent will probably ask you to make a decision on the spot. You should not do so for several reasons. Firstly, however good the first agent is, the next one might be even better. Having taken the trouble to compile a shortlist, you really should see everyone on it. Secondly, by delaying your decision for a couple of days you will get one last opportunity to test each agent's qualities of persistence and determination by seeing how vigorously they follow the appointment up. Thirdly, a number of important decisions have yet to be made about the terms and duration of the agency agreement. Such decisions are best not made under pressure.

At the end of the appointment thank the agent for his advice and say politely but firmly that you will be making a final decision within a few days. Most agents will accept this without further argument. The really effective agent, however, will not take no for an answer so easily and may try several more times to get a decision from you on the spot. This is an occasion when determination and persistence should be admired. The agent who tries hard to win your instructions is likely to be equally persistent when persuading potential purchasers to view your house.

The really skilled agent will seem to have an answer for every objection that you raise, for example:

Customer: I'd like to think it over.

Agent: Of course, but exactly what do you need to think about before deciding?

Customer: I've got one more agent to see.

Agent: Of course, but exactly what are you hoping they will offer which I don't?

It can be surprisingly difficult to resist a determined onslaught from a really good salesperson but resist you must. You cannot be sure of making the right decision under such pressure. The best way to counter such sales techniques is to keep repeating calmly but firmly that you will not make such an important decision on the spot.

Once the final agent has left, you are at last in a position to make your final decision. Often one agent will come out head and shoulders above the others. If this is not the case, it may be helpful to compare the best two or three agents using the comparison table at the end of this section.

Case study

Alan and Mary P asked three estate agents to value their property. All recommended quite similar asking prices so the decision came down to service and fee alone. Age 'A' quoted 1%, Agent 'B' quoted 1.5% and Agent 'C' 2%. Alan and Mary had some reservations about Agent 'A'. His office was in a back street, his advertising was sporadic and he did not have many boards up in their area. Nevertheless as he offered a saving on commission of £700 they decided to give him a go and signed a four week sole agency agreement.

After four weeks nothing much had happened, only two people had viewed the property and neither of them was in a position to proceed.

At this point John and Mary disinstructed Agent 'A' and instructed Agent 'C'. Agent 'C' had just sold another house in the street and had several interested applicants on his books. Seven viewings were arranged during the first week and the sale was agreed the following Monday.

Commenting on their experience Mary Smith said – 'It's clear now that Agent 'C' was far better equipped to find a buyer for our property and they were worth the extra fee. Agent 'A' just didn't have enough buyers. Thank goodness we only signed a four-week agency agreement'.

(16)

Exploring Agency Terms

COMMON AGENCY TERMS

Southern England

There are four types of agency agreement in use in southern England:

1. Sole agency

Sole agency means that just one agent is instructed to market a property. It is common these days for agents to ask for a minimum period of sole agency – an initial period of 8 to 12 weeks would be typical. If you choose to instruct an agent on a sole agency basis, you will probably be asked to sign a sole agency agreement. You should be aware that this is a legally binding contract which will prevent you from instructing any other agent during the sole agency period. If you break the agreement you may be liable to pay two lots of estate agents' commission, one to the original sole agent and one to the selling agent.

2. Joint sole agency

Joint sole agency means that two agents agree to share the agency commission regardless of which one of them achieves a sale. The most common circumstance for a joint sole agency agreement is where an expensive or unusual property needs to be marketed by a London agent in addition to a local one. Fee levels for joint sole

Agency are significantly higher than for a conventional sole agency.

3. Multiple agency
Multiple agency means that one or more agents are instructed to sell a property on the basis that whichever achieves a sale keeps the entire fee. Multiple agency is a very combative and inefficient way of doing business and because of this some agents will not accept instructions at all on this basis.

4. Sole selling rights
Sole selling rights work on a similar basis to sole agency. The difference is that the agent is entitled to receive a fee if the property is sold within the agency period *even if the agent was not responsible for achieving the sale*. If you sold your house to your brother, a fee would still technically be payable. If your property is going to be advertised on the Internet many agents will insist on a sole selling rights agreement.

Northern England
The agency system in northern England (defined as approximately north of Birmingham) operates in a different way. The four types of agency agreement detailed above are all available, but in northern England multiple agency agreements are much rarer. A second difference is that two types of sole agency agreement are in use.

1. Inclusive agency
Inclusive agency is the standard southern sole agency system where a fee is payable only if the property is sold.

2. Exclusive agency

Exclusive agency means that you will be liable to pay the agent's out-of-pocket expenses in addition to sales commission. These expenses will include items such as advertising, photography and the cost of erecting a 'For Sale' board. You will be liable to pay the agent's expenses *whether or not the property is sold.* You may also be liable to pay a withdrawal fee if the property is withdrawn from the market for any reason.

CHOOSING THE MOST APPROPRIATE TYPE OF AGENCY AGREEMENT

Southern England

Circumstances where a sole agency is appropriate
Sole agency has four important advantages over a multiple agency agreement:

1. **Cost**

   It is cheaper because as a sole agent has a greater chance of receiving a fee he can afford to charge a lower rate of commission. Sole agency fees are typically 20–50% lower than multiple agency rates.

2. **Service**

   You will usually get a better service; agents who are instructed on a multiple agency basis are often reluctant to spend money advertising and marketing a property which might be sold by a competitor. Your property will probably get far more exposure if you instruct an agent on a sole agency basis.

3. **Controlled exposure**

   No risk of overexposure, if a potential purchaser is offered the same property by ten different agents, he may wonder what is wrong with it. There is no doubt that overexposure can be counter-productive. A sole agency will avoid this problem.

4. **No conflict of interest**

   Imagine a situation where an agent receives a low offer for your property. If he is acting as your sole agent he can safely advise you to refuse it. If he is acting on a multiple agency basis he might be tempted to try to persuade you to accept the low offer to ensure that he gets the fee, not his competitor.

For these reasons I would advise most sellers to start off by instructing an agent on a sole agency basis. The exceptions are detailed below.

Circumstances where a joint sole agency is appropriate
People who are looking for a very expensive or unusual house are usually prepared to consider properties in a much larger geographical area than most ordinary purchasers.

A purchaser who wishes to buy a country estate, a listed property or perhaps a riverside property, might be prepared to look at anything within, say, two hours' travelling time of London. Such purchasers could not possibly register with all the agents in such a large area and most will therefore register their requirements only with agents in London and the major provincial cities.

Unless your property is being offered for sale at these locations it will be overlooked.

If your property is truly unusual, it is well worth the extra expense of a joint sole agency. If it is not, the extra commission payable (typically 30–50% more) is unlikely to be recovered.

Circumstances where a multiple agency is appropriate
Despite the inherent disadvantages of multiple agency there are some circumstances in which it might be appropriate:

1. **For village or suburban properties**
    Some village and suburban properties require exposure in more than one local town or centre. If you are selling a property in a village that is equidistant from three or more larger towns, you might consider instructing one agent in each centre on a multiple agency basis. Where there are only two local towns a joint sole agency agreement may be more appropriate.

2. **When no agent in the town is outstanding**
    Perhaps you can't make up your mind between instructing a small enthusiastic independent agent or a larger but apparently less efficient one. If you really can't decide, a multiple agency might be appropriate.

3. **When a property has already been unsuccessfully marketed by a sole agent**
    This is the most common reason for instructing an agent on a multiple agency basis. Although multiple

agency is often appropriate in these circumstances, you should also consider sacking the first agent and entering into a second sole agency agreement with another firm.

The one thing to avoid at all costs is the temptation to instruct every agent in the town. In a town with 20 agents there is nothing to be gained from instructing more than two or three. If you instruct all twenty, your property will be overexposed and your chances of selling it seriously reduced.

Northern England

Circumstances where an exclusive sole agency is appropriate
As an exclusive agency client you will be responsible for paying all out-of- pocket expenses involved with marketing your property whether it is sold or not. As an inclusive agency client you will, through higher fee levels, end up paying not only the costs of marketing your property, but also a proportion of the cost of marketing other properties that were withdrawn from the market leaving the agent with unrecoverable costs to bear. For this reason exclusive agency is usually the most cost-effective choice for the committed vendor.

Circumstances where an inclusive sole agency is appropriate
There are two circumstances where an inclusive agency might be appropriate:

1. When you are not certain about an agent's ability.

2. Where there is a chance that you might change your mind about moving. (In which case is it really fair to waste the agent's time and money?)

INSTRUCTING AN ESTATE AGENT

Having made your decision regarding which agent to instruct and on what terms, you should next clarify in your mind your detailed instructions to that agent. In particular you need to make a decision on:

Initial asking price

Bearing in mind all the evidence that you have seen and heard, are you certain about your initial asking price? If it is too high, it will spoil the momentum of the marketing campaign and may demotivate the agent. On the other hand, if it is too low, it will be all but impossible to raise it later.

Period of sole agency

What period of sole agency are you prepared to give? If it is too short (say less than six weeks) the agent may be reluctant to spend money marketing a property that he might not sell. If it is too long (say more than 12 weeks) you run the risk of being tied to an ineffective agent.

Subagencies

Some agents will invite other agents in the town to act on a subagency basis. This means that they will also offer your property for sale and if they sell it will receive half the commission. My opinion is that subagencies are usually not in the best interests of the seller, mainly because of the risk of overexposure. If you are prepared to allow your agent to instruct subagents, you should insist that the number is strictly limited and ask for a list of all subagents before they are instructed.

'For Sale' board

Approximately 25% of all applicants are attracted by 'For Sale' boards and a board will therefore undoubtedly increase your chances of selling. If you are reluctant to have one, you should examine your objections most carefully. Is the risk of the odd unwanted caller a price worth paying for a quicker sale?

Keys

If at all possible you should give your agent a key. This is even more important if you are out at work in the daytime. A surprising number of people wish to view during working hours and many will not bother to try to make another appointment if they cannot view immediately.

Having made a decision on all the above issues you are now ready to telephone the lucky agent to inform him of your decision and arrange a final appointment to put the house on the market.

Informing the unsuccessful agents

It is well worth spending five or ten minutes telephoning or writing to the unsuccessful agents to inform them of your decision. You might need their services in the future and a short courtesy call at this time will make it far easier to go back to them in the future should the need arise.

THE SOLE AGENCY AGREEMENT

The agency agreement is a legal contract and you should read it most carefully before signing. You should not hesitate to ask the agent to explain any clause that is unclear. If you are not happy with any aspect of the agreement you should refuse to sign it on the spot and take it to your solicitor or to a trusted friend for clarification.

A typical agency agreement will include the following:

1. **Confirmation of fee level**
   Check that this is what has been agreed. Also check any multiple agency rate. It will be far easier to negotiate a multiple agency rate now, when the sole agency period is being agreed, than later when it is being ended.

2. **Confirmation of asking price**
   Double check the figure agreed.

3. **Confirmation of agency terms**
   Check that you are signing for a sole or multiple agency as appropriate.

4. **Sole agency period**
   Check that this is as agreed. Check also whether a notice period is hidden in the small print.

5. **Authority to pay fees**
   Many agency agreements contain a clause that gives your solicitor authority to pay the agent's fees from the sale proceeds.

6. **Offer of 'connected services'**
   Estate agents must by law inform you of any service that might be offered to potential purchasers such as mortgage advice, removals or the sale of their own property.

7. **'For Sale' board**

   Many agency agreements include a clause authorising the erection of a For Sale board. Delete this clause if you don't want one.

8. **Race Relations Act**

   Many agreements include a clause that confirms that you will not discriminate against potential purchasers on account of their colour or race.

9. **Subagencies**

   Many agreements include a clause that gives the agent authority to instruct subagents. Delete this if appropriate.

10. **Property Misdescriptions Act**

    You may be asked to sign a separate form relating to the Property Misdescriptions Act.

11. **Other specific instructions**

    You should insist that any additional instructions given to the agent are recorded in writing on the sole agency agreement to prevent misunderstandings.

Case study

James and Tina K were in a great hurry to sell their flat in London so they decided to instruct three agents on a multiple-agency basis. This tactic seemed to pay off and ten viewings were arranged for the first weekend. The problems started on Monday when all three agents said that they had a buyer who was prepared to offer the full asking price.

James and Tina asked for details about the position of each buyer and on the basis of what they were told they decided to accept an offer from a nice young couple who had sold their own property and said that they would be ready to exchange contracts within three weeks.

Five weeks later little progress had been made so James and Tina asked their solicitor to investigate the reason for the delay. He made enquiries and reported back that the nice young couple had lost the buyer for their own property and were trying to find another. Their sale had in fact fallen through nearly five weeks ago.

James and Tina were furious. They rang their agent and accused him of not supervising the sale closely enough. Their agent replied that it was not his fault if someone told him lies. James and Tina withdrew from the sale and sold instead through another agent to one of the other people who had made an offer five weeks previously. They were left with a bill for abortive costs of nearly £400.

James and Tina suspect that their first agent deliberately withheld information about their buyer's sale falling through because he did not want to risk losing his commission, but they know that they will never be able to prove this.

Commenting on his experience James said 'Next time we will instruct just one agent, then we will know that they are acting in our interest not theirs'.

(17)

Finding a Buyer

PREPARING THE PARTICULARS

The first thing that your estate agent will do after instructions have been confirmed is to prepare the property particulars.

The particulars will play an extremely important role in persuading potential purchasers to view your property. It is, therefore, worth going to some considerable trouble to ensure that they show the property to its best advantage.

The following tips will help to ensure that your particulars stand out from the crowd:

General layout

The typical purchaser will receive several dozen sets of particulars during his property search. Because of this, your particulars will need to make their impact within just a few seconds. Sloppy photocopying or poor layout will reduce significantly the number of potential buyers that decide to view and should not be tolerated.

Photography

Ninety per cent of purchasers will look at the photograph before they look at anything else. If they don't like what they see, they will reject your property out of hand. It is therefore vital to ensure that the photograph shows your property in the very best possible light.

1. Choosing an angle
The angle that the photograph is taken from should be chosen with particular care. Most photographs show the front elevation. However, if your property looks better from another angle, there is no reason why the photograph should not show the back or the side.

2. Colour v. black and white
The photograph itself really should be in colour. If your estate agent does not use colour photographs on his details, it is worth considering paying the extra cost of colour photography yourself.

3. Size
The size of the photograph is important. A photograph that measures 5×7in. or larger will make a far greater impact than the traditional mini print.

4. Recentness
The last point to make about the external photograph is that it must be recent. A photograph of a property covered in snow, sent out in August, will convey the message 'and they *still* haven't sold it!'

5. Internal photographs
Internal photographs can play a useful role in persuading people to view a property. If your property has any particularly attractive internal features, you should ask your estate agent to include an internal photograph on the details.

6. Photographing ugly properties

Some houses are not particularly photogenic. Some houses are just plain ugly. If your property falls into this category (be honest with yourself here) it may be better to include only internal photographs on the property particulars.

The text

You must always remember that the purpose of the property particulars is to persuade people to view your property, not to sell the property itself. You should therefore be ruthless about removing from the text all unnecessary information. In particular you should take care to remove any trivial details that might discourage people from viewing. For example, reference to a pink bathroom suite would do nothing to increase a property's saleability but could very easily put some purchasers off.

PROPERTY PARTICULARS AND THE LAW

Estate agents used to be famous for their ability to make even the most undesirable property sound like a palace. All such hyperbole was ended by the passing of the Property Misdescriptions Act in April 1993.

The Property Misdescriptions Act made it a *criminal* offence for an estate agent (but not a home owner) to misdescribe a property that is offered for sale. The penalties for non-compliance are severe and even a minor transgression can lead to a substantial fine and a criminal record for the estate agent.

The passing of the Property Misdescriptions Act has led to far-reaching changes in estate agency practice and this has affected vendors in two ways. The first effect of the act is that estate agents' details have become far shorter and less colourful than they used to be. Estate agents dare not make any statement that cannot be verified. Thus a phrase such as 'the house is ten minutes walk from the shops' has either been changed to 'the property is 637m from the nearest shop' or, more commonly, omitted altogether.

The second effect of the act has been to cause considerable delays in putting properties onto the market. The reason for this is that estate agents now have a statutory obligation to verify all claims that they wish to make about a property. For example, if a property has been rewired the agent will need to see a detailed invoice for the work. If a property has damp guarantees the agent will need to see a copy of the guarantee. If a property has a 67-year lease, the agent will need to see a copy of the lease to verify this. Many homeowners do not have such documents readily available and the delays that occur whilst the documents are obtained can cause considerable inconvenience and frustration. If you find yourself in this situation, you will need to make a choice between waiting for the documents to be obtained, and marketing your property with all references to the unsubstantiated facts omitted from the details.

GETTING PEOPLE TO VIEW

Once the house is on the market your agent should start earning his fee by persuading as many people as possible to view it. He will try to achieve this in a number of ways:

By telephone

The agent should have a number of 'hot applicants' on his register. These are people who are prepared to view without seeing the details and are in a position to proceed with a purchase immediately. (First-time buyers or own property sold.) The agent should telephone these people to obtain viewings *before* the details are sent out. These are the hottest applicants of all. One of them may wish to buy your property immediately.

Via the Internet

Your property should immediately be added to your agent's website and uploaded to the major property portals.

By post

During the preceding two to three months the agent's general marketing campaign should have attracted a number of applicants. Within the first few days, the agent should send a set of particulars to every applicant that he has in the price range. Sending details alone is not enough. The effective agent will also telephone each of these applicants a few days after they receive the details to obtain feedback and to attempt to persuade them to view.

Circulating details to other branches

If you have instructed a multi-office agent, details of your property should be circulated to all the neighbouring branches. This will not always happen automatically. Inter-branch rivalry often means that neighbouring branches end up competing with each other rather than co-operating. You must ensure that such inter-branch rivalries do not affect your chances of obtaining a sale.

You can check this by doing two things. Firstly, ask what commission sharing arrangements are in place in the event of your property being sold by another branch (do they seem fair to you?). Secondly, try phoning the neighbouring branches posing as an applicant looking for a property in the same price range as yours and see whether your property is mentioned.

Erection of a 'For Sale' board

A 'For Sale' board is an important marketing tool. Something like a quarter of all sales are achieved due to a board. If you really want to sell your house for the best possible price in the shortest possible time, then you need a 'For Sale' board. The board may encourage the odd unwanted visitor to knock on the door without an appointment, but such people can easily be turned away and this small intrusion is a price well worth paying for the extra interest that a board will generate.

HOW LONG SHOULD IT TAKE TO FIND A BUYER?

It is, of course, impossible to predict how long it will take to find a buyer. However, statistically the time when a property in southern England is most likely to sell is during the first four weeks of going onto the market. During this period the agent is able to work on all the potential buyers who have registered during the preceding few months. By the end of the first month you should certainly have had a number of viewings and you may well have achieved a sale. If you have not, you should begin to consider the possibility that your property is going to prove more difficult to sell than you thought.

In many parts of northern England the market tends to operate more slowly. If you are selling a property in the north you should allow 8 to 12 weeks for the initial marketing campaign to run its course.

If you have not achieved a sale within these timescales, you should begin to consider the possibility that your property is going to prove more difficult to sell than you first thought.

RUNNING THE ADVERTISING CAMPAIGN

The advertising campaign is a very important part of the overall marketing plan. The following hints will help to ensure that you get maximum benefit from the advertisements that are run for your property:

Page position

Certain positions on the page attract far more interest than others. In general terms the rules are:

- ◆ Right-hand pages are better than left-hand pages.
- ◆ The top of the page is better than the bottom of the page.
- ◆ The boxes at the edge of a page get more interest than those in the centre of the page.

This can be shown as a diagram (see Figure 14).

Try to insist on a good position when your property is advertised. A good position could double or treble the response.

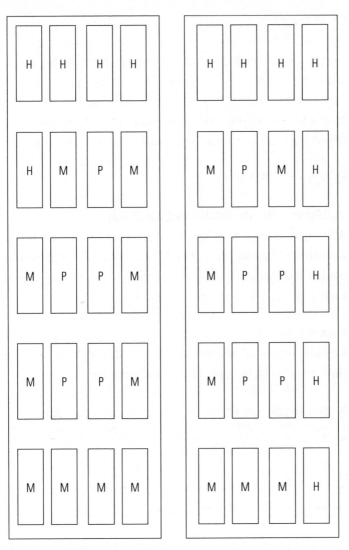

H = High response
M = Medium response
P = Poor response

Figure 14. The best (and worst) positions for your advertisement.

The photograph

Potential buyers will look at the photograph and decide whether or not they want to view the property within seconds. It is therefore essential to choose a photograph that shows the property in its best light. If you have any reservations about the photograph you should not hesitate to ask your agent to take another one.

Subsequent photographs

Many buyers have a memory like an elephant for houses that have been previously advertised. If they recognise a photograph that they have seen before, they will move straight on to the next property without even pausing to read the text.

The golden rule therefore is never to use the same photograph twice. Subsequent advertisements should use a photograph taken from a different angle, an internal shot or perhaps a rear view of the property.

Advertising an ugly property

There is little point in photographing an ugly property. If your house looks like a concrete prison block you should consider:

♦ Advertising it with an internal photograph.

♦ Advertising it without a photograph at all.

♦ Asking your agent to advertise a prettier property in the same price range as your own on the understanding that all respondents will be told about your property as well as the one advertised.

The text

The purpose of an advertisement is to generate enquiries. If everything that a potential purchaser needs to know about the property is included in the advertisement then they will have no reason to contact the agent. The effective agent will counter this by withholding a vital piece of information about each property. This might be the location, the price or the number of bedrooms.

By advertising in this way, the agent can increase quite significantly the number of enquiries that each advertisement generates. Once a prospective purchaser is on the phone the agent will have a much better chance of persuading him to view the property.

Text of subsequent advertisements

An advertisement that has been run once is stale. If the same advertisement is run again it will achieve a much reduced response. You should, therefore, never use the same text twice. Subsequent advertisements should be rewritten from scratch and should highlight different features of the property. (See Figure 15.)

Setting an advertising budget

In southern England, the cost of local property advertising is usually included in the agency fee. In northern England many agents charge for all advertising and will want to agree an advertising budget with you at the time of instruction.

You should be aware that many agents make a profit from selling you advertising space and therefore have an incentive to sell you as much as possible. You should be

First advertisement Appeals to family with children	Close to Queens School This three-bedroom semi-detached property is situated in a quiet cul-de-sac and is very convenient to Queens School. It has three bedrooms and a 60ft south-facing garden. Price £69,950
Second advertisement Appeals to professional couple	First-class commuter access This three-bedroom semi-detached property is within two minutes of the M1, Junction 10 and less than half a mile from the mainline station. The accommodation comprises three bedrooms and two separate reception rooms. The property is in excellent condition throughout. Price £69,950
Third advertisement Appeals to gardeners	South-facing garden This three-bedroom, two reception property is in first-class condition throughout. A particular feature is the well-stocked 60ft south facing garden which has been lovingly tended by the present owners. Price £69,950.

Figure 15. Rewriting your advertisement
to attract a different response.

cautious about agreeing to a major advertising campaign straight away. For most properties a budget that covers three or four local advertisements should be sufficient. If necessary, the budget can always be reviewed at a later date.

National advertising

For most properties a local advertising campaign will be sufficient. However, some properties will benefit from further exposure in a regional, national or specialist publication. Such properties might include:

- High-value properties.

- Waterside properties.

- Properties with equestrian facilities.

- Properties that might have an appeal as a holiday home.

- Highly unusual/individual properties.

- Properties with potential for dual residential/commercial usage.

- Properties with investment/lettings potential.

If your property falls into one of these categories, you should ask your agent to advise you on the cost of an advertising campaign in the appropriate publications. The cost of such advertising is nearly always borne by the vendor, not the agent.

Editorial coverage

Most local property newspapers have an editorial section

which features a small number of properties each week. Most papers give each of the agents space in the editorial section on a rota basis. Editorials often generate far more enquiries for a property than an ordinary advertisement and it would be well worth trying to persuade your agent to include your property in their next editorial feature.

Open house

A more unconventional approach to advertising is the open house. For some reason many purchasers are far more willing to attend an open house than to arrange a specific appointment to view a property. Perhaps they feel under less pressure. Perhaps they don't want to commit themselves to a precise time. Whatever the reason, advertising an open house can generate far more interest than a conventional advertisement.

The house is advertised as usual except that the times of the open house are prominently displayed. Some open house advertisements include the full address. In other cases the address is withheld so that the agent can take the applicant's details and verify them to be genuine prior to the appointment.

'Coming soon' advertisements

A variation on the open house idea is the 'coming soon' advertisement. This is effectively a teaser campaign. Advertisements appear over a period of two to three weeks. (See Figure 16.)

> **Coming Soon**
> Four-bedroom detached property in Lincoln's Fields area. The
> property is in need of some updating and refurbishment.
> Price guide £100,000.

Figure 16. A 'coming soon' advertisement.

Buyers who respond to the advertisement are all invited
to view the property on a predetermined day at a
predetermined time. No one is allowed to see the property
until this time. The effect of several buyers arriving at
once is that the property appears to be in great demand.
As a result it is often possible to achieve a premium price.

SHOWING PEOPLE AROUND

Who should conduct the viewings?

An estate agent will nearly always show a house more
effectively than the owner could themselves. There are two
reasons for this:

♦ Purchasers are more likely to tell the agent what they
  really think of a property. This feedback helps the
  agent to overcome objections.

♦ Experience will have taught the agent how to show
  each property to its best advantage.

You should therefore ask your agent to accompany as
many viewings as possible, even if they are at a time when
you will be at home yourselves.

Preparing for a viewing

A well-conducted viewing should aim to appeal to all the senses:

Sight

◆ Try to ensure that the house is as tidy as possible.

◆ Draw all the curtains right back from the windows to make the rooms appear bigger and brighter.

◆ On dull days turn all the lights on – electric light is much warmer and more friendly than daylight (although sunlight is best of all).

◆ In spring, autumn or winter light a fire if you have one.

Sound

◆ Turn the television off. It makes people feel that they are intruding.

◆ Put some background music on quietly (classical is best).

◆ Close the windows if the house is affected by any sort of background noise (traffic, trains, etc.).

◆ A barking dog is for many people a most unpleasant first impression of the property. Try to take the dog out for a walk when a viewing is expected. If that is not possible, shut the dog in the car or in a back room until the potential purchasers have left.

Smell

◆ Attractive smells can make a very positive impression – coffee brewing, bread baking, food cooking are all homely and atmospheric.

♦ Unpleasant smells can be very off-putting; these
   include dogs, tobacco, air fresheners and dirty bins.

Atmosphere

I was once told a story about a beautiful flat that had
failed to sell after more than a hundred viewings.
Eventually the agent discovered that the reason was that
the vendors (who were divorcing) were showing purchasers round in an atmosphere that was so poisonous that all
they wanted to do was get out. By conducting viewings
whilst the vendors were out the agent was able to obtain
an offer within a few days.

When the agent is conducting the viewing

If the agent is conducting the viewing the best thing that
you can do is to go out. If that is not possible, the next
best thing is to stay out of the way (preferably in one of
the less attractive rooms) until the agent has left. The
agent will introduce you to the purchasers when they view
the room that you are in but otherwise it is best for you to
play no part in the proceedings.

Conducting a viewing yourself

The following hints will help you to make the best of every
viewing:

1. Preparation

Ask the agent about the purchaser's background – their
job, hobbies, etc. It is much easier to strike up a
conversation with someone when you know something
about them. Ask the agent also about the purchaser's
main requirements (e.g. large garden, lots of space
downstairs, low maintenance, etc.). This will enable you

to stress these key points during the viewing.

2. Greeting
First impressions really do count. Smile when you greet the purchasers – it can make a real difference.

3. One of you or two
Only one of you should conduct the viewing. Your partner will only get in the way and make the rooms seem smaller.

4. Order of rooms
Show the buyer the best room first. Take them round the rest of the house in a logical order then end up in the best room again at the end. This will mean that their first and last impression is a good one.

5. After you
A room always seems bigger when it is empty. You should therefore always let purchasers enter each room first.

6. Don't talk too much
Many vendors, perhaps through nervousness, point out every power point and dimmer switch. This can be most off-putting. It's really best to say as little as possible. You should, however:

◆ Relate the house to the purchaser's requirements, e.g. 'I understand you wanted a big garden. This is one third of an acre'.

◆ Point out things the purchasers might not notice themselves, e.g. you could knock the pantry through to make a breakfast area here.

Create a warm atmosphere by saying things like how happy you have been in the house.

7. Privacy
Couples need time alone to discuss the house before they leave. The best way to achieve this is to send them out to look at the garden on their own.

8. Security
These days you cannot be too careful. I was once told a story about a purchaser with several million pounds to spend, who was seen to steal a bottle of perfume during an accompanied viewing. Keep your eyes open and never leave purchasers alone in the house.

9. Handling questions
Be cautious about answering questions like 'Why are you moving?' It is so easy to put purchasers off.

10. Dealing with rude people
You may meet someone who spends the whole visit being rude about your house. It really is best to ignore such comments unless the provocation is extreme. Some people are just rude by nature. Others may actually be interested in the property and might be trying to talk the price down.

11. Handling offers
On no account should you get embroiled in price negotiations yourself. It is so easy to say something that you later regret. If a purchaser makes an offer, whatever it is, thank them enthusiastically and refer them to the agent.

12. At the end of the viewing

However disinterested the purchasers appear, end the viewing by offering them a chance to go round again and/ or to come back for a second look.

13. Obtaining feedback

The agent should let you know what every purchaser thought within 48 hours of the viewing. If they do not, ring them.

14. Prepare for disappointments

Purchasers are often quite nervous when they are viewing someone's house and some cover up this nervousness by saying how lovely everything is. This doesn't mean they want to buy it. Be prepared to find that many promising viewings do not result in an offer.

15. Maintain your enthusiasm

No matter how many people you have shown round, it is vital to maintain your enthusiasm. I have known of many cases where houses have failed to sell because their owners (or agents) have grown sick of showing people around. If you do not seem interested in selling the property no purchaser will wish to buy it.

Case study

Lydia W was horrified to see the way in which her agent had prepared particulars of her property. The photograph was in black and white not colour as she had been promised and it was taken from a most unattractive angle that made her property appear far smaller than it really was. No wonder she had had so few viewings.

Lydia complained to her estate agent who took a new photograph, added some internal shots and produced the full colour details that she had been promised. The number of viewings increased immediately and an offer was agreed two weeks later.

(18)

Reviewing Progress

ARRANGING THE FIRST REVIEW MEETING

Your house has been on the market for about four weeks (eight weeks in the north). It has been advertised, details have been sent out, and purchasers have been telephoned. You may well have had some viewings but there is still no sign of a buyer.

If this is the stage that you have reached, then it is time to visit your agent for a review meeting. Telephone your agent, tell him that you are concerned that the property has not yet sold and ask for an appointment to discuss what else can be done. Try not to get drawn into a discussion over the telephone. A review meeting really is something that needs to handled face to face.

HAS THE PROPERTY BEEN PROPERLY MARKETED?

Start the review meeting by asking your agent, in a non-confrontational way, why he thinks that your property has not yet sold. Whatever answer he gives, you should ask him next to go through everything that he has already done to find a buyer. In particular you should ask about:

1. **Feedback from existing viewings** – what comments have been made by the people who have viewed? Is there one thing that is putting people off? Could anything be done to change it?

2. **Mail-outs** – ask how many sets of details have been sent out.

3. **Phone-outs** – ask how many people have been telephoned to try to obtain a viewing. Ask what comments were made about the property by people who did not wish to view it. Again, is one thing putting people off? Could something be done to change it?

4. **Other branches** – check to ensure that any other local branches have details of your property.

5. **Advertising** – ask to see copies of all advertisements for your property. Are you satisfied these show your property to the best advantage?

6. **Details** – ask to see a copy of the details again. Are they still as well presented as the first set you saw?

REVIEWING THE ASKING PRICE

The value of any property is ultimately determined by the price of the properties that are currently competing for the same buyers. The properties that are available change all the time and this means that the value of your property can fluctuate. If, for example, the house next door to you is put on the market for £5,000 less than yours, it will make it much more difficult to achieve your asking price. In order to check that your asking price is still realistic you should:

◆ Ask to see full details of all houses that the agent has sold in the same price range, whilst your property has been on the market. How do they compare to your own?

- Ask to see details of all other houses that the agent is currently marketing in the same price range. These properties will be competing directly with yours for the same buyers. How do they compare?

- Go through the current issue of the property newspaper with your agent. Are any of the properties advertised by other agents better value than your own?

In the light of such evidence you may need to consider reducing the asking price.

WHAT ELSE COULD BE DONE TO FIND A BUYER?

If you are certain that the asking price is correct, you might ask your agent to take all or some of the following actions:

- Prepare new particulars. By taking new photographs and rewriting the particulars an old property can be made to seem like a new instruction. Sometimes this will result in viewings from people who were put off by something in the original particulars.

- Ask the agent to send every member of his sales team to see your property. They may be more enthusiastic about selling a property that they have seen themselves.

- Readvertise – try to find a different aspect to feature, perhaps the garden, the history of the house, anything to make it appeal to a different group of purchasers.

- Consider national or regional advertising. For many properties national advertising produces disappointing results. However, it might be worth considering one advert to test the market in a larger geographical area.

◆ Increase the incentive. Consider offering a bonus of say 2% to the individual negotiator who sells the property. This can transform their motivation! You will need the approval of the branch manager or proprietor.

Changing agents

You may discover during the review meeting that your agent has not been doing his job effectively. If this is the case, you must tell him why you are dissatisfied. This is not a time to beat about the bush.

Four weeks is probably too soon to consider changing agents but, if you have good cause for dissatisfaction, it might be the best thing to do. However, before you disinstruct your agent, you should check carefully the terms of any sole agency agreement that you have signed. If you do not, you could find yourself liable to pay two lots of agency fees.

DECIDING WHAT TO DO IF IT STILL WON'T SELL

Around eight weeks (16 in the North) have passed and there is still no sign of a buyer. What should be done next?

Arrange a second review meeting

The first thing to do is to arrange a second review meeting with the estate agent. This should be conducted in a very similar way to the first one:

◆ Ask the agent why he thinks your property hasn't sold.

◆ Ask what comments have been made by people who have viewed – is one thing putting them off?

◆ Ask how many sets of details have been sent out.

- Ask how many people have been told about the house on the telephone.

- Ask what comments have been made by buyers who did not want to view, having seen the details. Is one thing putting them off?

- Check that the property has been circulated to any other local branches.

- Ask to see copies of advertising for the property run since the last review meeting.

- Ask to see a copy of the details again.

- Ask the agent again if he will accompany all viewings if he is not already doing so.

- Consider rewriting the details if you have not already done so.

- Consider a 'For Sale' board if you don't already have one.

- Consider an open house, if you haven't already tried one.

- Ask the agent to send every member of the sales team to view the house for themselves.

Reviewing the asking price

If the property has not sold after eight weeks it could well be that the asking price is too high. Try to assess this by:

- Asking to see details of all other properties in the same price range as yours.

- Asking to see details of properties that the agent has

sold in the same price range since the last review meeting.

◆ Looking at the price of any similar properties to your own that have been advertised in the newspaper.

Try to be honest with yourself and ask how your property compares to the competition.

CHECKING UP ON YOUR AGENT

If you are certain that the asking price is realistic, the next thing to do is check up on how well your agent is marketing your property. This can be done in a number of ways:

◆ Ask a friend to register with your agent as a buyer for a property like yours. What sort of service do they get? Is your property promoted both on the telephone and by the sending out of written particulars?

◆ Ask your friend to arrange to actually view your property with your estate agent. How well do they feel that the property is being sold?

◆ Phone the agent yourself to enquire about a property that has been advertised at a similar price to your own. Is your property also mentioned?

◆ Phone the agent and say that you have seen the 'For Sale' board outside your house. Does the agent really push hard to try to get a viewing?

If such tests reveal that your property is still being effectively marketed then there is no alternative but to be patient. If not the time may have come to change agents.

Case study

Sanjay and Monisha P had been trying to sell their five-bedroom property in the Midlands for three months without success. They could not understand why their property had failed to sell so they arranged a review meeting with their agent. They were horrified by what they found.

The particulars which had originally been full colour photographs now had a poor quality black-and-white photocopy of the original photographs. When they asked their agent what the viewers had said about their house it was clear that he had never bothered to follow the viewings up so he did not know. Furthermore the national advertisement that they had been promised had not been run.

Sanjay and Monisha made their dissatisfaction clear and told their agent that if he did not address their concerns immediately they would withdraw their property.

Their agent took a new photograph, prepared particulars, sent them out to everyone on the mailing list again and followed up with a phone call. Within two weeks nine viewings had been arranged and an offer had been agreed at close to the asking price.

19

Changing Your Estate Agent

The time may come when you have to accept that your first agent is not going to find a buyer within a reasonable period of time.

Once you reach this point, the first decision to make is whether to instruct a second agent as well as or instead of the first one.

CONSIDERING SOLE AGENCY V. MULTIPLE AGENCY
The main arguments are:

- Multiple agency encourages agents to work for themselves, not for you.

- Overexposure of the property can reduce the chances of finding a buyer.

- Multiple agency is more expensive.

- A sole agent has more incentive to work harder to achieve a sale.

For all these reasons the best course of action in most situations is to disinstruct (withdraw your instructions from) the first agent and to appoint the new agent on a sole agency basis.

DISINSTRUCTING AN AGENT

Disinstructing an agent is probably best done over the telephone. Thank the agent for his work in trying to find a buyer and tell him that you are sorry that he was not successful. Then tell him politely, but firmly, that you will now be instructing another agent and that you would like him to take the property off his books. You should expect the agent to try to persuade you to stick with him for a little longer and he may even offer incentives, such as extra advertising, to persuade you to do so. You should not be swayed.

Contractual obligations

Your sole agency agreement may impose contractual obligations on you and you should check it carefully before disinstructing your agent. Common obligations would be:

- A notice period for disinstructing (typically two weeks) may be required.

- Withdrawal fee – many agents, particularly in the north of England, will charge a withdrawal fee if they are disinstructed for any reason. This could be several hundred pounds.

- Out-of-pocket expenses – many agents, again particularly in the north of England, require reimbursement of all outstanding expenses such as advertising, colour photography etc. at the time of disinstruction.

BREAKING A SOLE AGENCY AGREEMENT

If you granted the agent a period of sole agency you will usually be contractually obliged to honour it. If the property is sold by another agent within the sole agency period you could find yourself liable to pay two agency fees. You might try to persuade the original agent to release you from the agency agreement by pointing out that he has nothing to gain from keeping a dissatisfied vendor on his books. However, the agent is not obliged to release you from the agreement early and if he will not, you have no choice but to delay instructing the new agent until after the original agreement has expired.

AVOIDING COMMISSION DISPUTES

A fee will be payable to the first agent in the event that the property is sold to a buyer who has previously viewed it through that agent. To avoid arguments in the future it is as well to write to your agent to ask him to do two things:

◆ To confirm that he has taken the property off the market.

◆ To provide a list of the names of all purchasers who have viewed through him.

INSTRUCTING A SECOND AGENT

Choosing an agent

The most obvious agent to instruct the second time round will be the runner-up in your original beauty contest. However, this decision should not be an automatic one. If another agent has sold a lot of houses in your area during the time that yours has been on the market, then it would be well worth asking that agent to value your property before you make a final decision.

Booking the appointment

All the local agents will know that your property has been on the market and there is nothing to gain from trying to hide this. However, it is important that the agent should not think that the appointment is a guaranteed instruction. If he does he may send a junior member of staff to take the details. To avoid this you should tell him on the phone that:

♦ You wish to instruct a new agent on a sole not a multiple agency basis.

♦ You need advice on the asking price and would like to see details of similar properties in the same price range (both sold and available).

Preparing for the appointment

You should prepare for the agent's visit in the same way as you would for any other viewing. Agents are human too, and their valuation will be affected by how well the property is presented.

Establishing the ground rules

The agent will often expect an appointment at a house that is already on the market to be a guaranteed instruction. You should make it clear at the beginning of the appointment that this is not the case. Tell the agent that you are disappointed that the first company that you instructed did not find a buyer and that you are anxious not to make another mistake.

The agent's sales presentation

Having agreed on an asking price, the next stage is to ask the agent what he will do differently from the first agent to market your property. In particular ask him:

- How he will present the particulars differently.
- How and where he will advertise.
- How many purchasers he has on his books.
- Why he thinks the house has not sold already.
- What other properties have recently sold in the same price range.

Negotiating a fee

You will be in a weaker position to negotiate a fee than you were the last time around. The agent will know that your property has proved to be difficult to sell and will therefore quite probably hold out for a higher fee. However, this does not mean that you have to accept whatever fee is offered. You might suggest that you have an alternative agent in mind who you will instruct if an agreement cannot be reached.

The sole agency contract

Don't be pressurised into signing an agreement on the spot. If you have any doubts ask the agent to leave the agreement with you.

The sole agency period

The period of sole agency should be similar to the period given to the original agent – eight weeks would be typical. Any less and the agent will be reluctant to spend money marketing a property that he may not sell. Any more and you run the risk of being stuck with an ineffective agent.

Instructing an agent on a multiple agency basis

There are circumstances where it is appropriate to

instruct a second agent on a multiple basis. Perhaps the second agent is based in another town or suburb or advertises in a different newspaper. However, a third agent will very seldom do anything to increase your chances and a fourth or fifth may actually make it more difficult to find a buyer. However desperate you are to sell I would urge you not to overexpose the property.

WHAT TO DO IF IT STILL WON'T SELL

Hard as it is to accept, you have now done everything that can be done. If you are not willing or able to be patient, the only thing left to do is to begin reducing the asking price until you reach the figure at which the property sells immediately. Be warned, this could be many thousands of pounds less than its true value.

Case study

Stuart and Linda J were very disappointed with their original estate agent. When they went to see him to find out why their property had not sold it quickly became clear that he had not been doing his job properly. Stuart and Linda felt badly let down and gave their agent notice that they would be terminating their sole agency agreement when it expired.

Their second agent was by comparison a model of efficiency. The details were better, they had a much more proactive approach to persuading people to view on the telephone and they phoned the next day to report on the feedback from each viewing.

Within a week an offer had been agreed. Stuart and Linda were amused to find that their buyer had also been registered with the original agent who had failed to either send them details or contact them by telephone – poetic justice indeed.

(20)

Dealing With Offers

PREPARING TO NEGOTIATE

At last the moment you have been waiting for has arrived – you have received an offer. Unfortunately you cannot afford to breathe a sigh of relief just yet. A great deal of care will still be necessary in order to ensure that the best possible selling price is achieved and that the sale goes through to a successful completion. Three general principles will help to ensure that your negotiations have the very best chance of reaching a satisfactory conclusion:

Don't handle negotiations yourself

Whatever the temptation, you should never handle negotiations yourself. Your estate agent will be able to negotiate an offer more effectively than you for a number of reasons.

1. **Experience** – your agent has the experience of having negotiated many other sales before.

2. **Emotional involvement** – the agent should be able to negotiate in a calm and businesslike fashion without the burden of emotional involvement.

3. **Extra thinking time** – direct negotiations often mean that you are forced into giving an answer or making a concession on the spot. By negotiating through a third

party, who does not have the authority to reach a binding agreement on your behalf, you buy invaluable thinking time.

An astute buyer will know that he will be better off by negotiating directly with the vendor and may try to apply considerable pressure in an attempt to persuade you not to involve the agent in the negotiations. You should not give in to such tactics. Doing so could cost you thousands of pounds.

Don't take offence at low offers

Under the Estate Agents Act, an estate agent must inform you of every offer that he receives for your property immediately and in writing. Should you receive what you consider to be an insulting offer for your property, don't shoot the messenger. Your agent is only complying with his statutory duty.

The receipt of frequent low offers is also evidence that the agent is doing his job effectively by asking everyone who views the property if there is any price at which they would be interested in buying. This type of closing question does occasionally result in a sale to a purchaser who is embarrassed about making a low offer. Unfortunately, it also produces a number of low offers.

Conduct negotiations in writing

Negotiations should be conducted in writing or by fax wherever possible. This will ensure that your position is not misrepresented and will save a lot of unnecessary arguments about exactly what was agreed later on.

ESTABLISHING IF THE BUYER CAN PROCEED

Before you even begin to discuss the issue of price, it is vital to find out about your potential buyer's ability to proceed. Vital questions to ask include:

- The buyer's ideal timescale.
- The reason for the move.
- Has the buyer got property to sell?
- If so, has that property been sold?
- If so, what stage has the sale reached?
- Are there any other dependent transactions in the chain?
- If so, exactly what stage has each transaction reached?
- Will the buyer require a mortgage?
- If so, what percentage of the purchase price will the mortgage be for?
- Which mortgage lender does the buyer intend to use?

You should be extremely wary about dealing with any buyer who cannot or will not answer these essential questions.

WEIGHING UP THE OFFER

Whilst price will usually be the most important factor, speed and certainty will also be important to most sellers. An offer that is slow to complete could cost you an extra mortgage payment or might even result in you losing your purchase. You should also remember that an offer that falls through will, apart from the disappointment, also cost you a substantial amount of money in wasted legal and survey fees.

Factors that could prevent a buyer from completing his purchase quickly and smoothly might include:

Length of chain
Every additional transaction in the chain increases the chances of something going wrong. You should be looking for someone with the shortest possible chain. Purchasers with nothing to sell are best of all.

Size of mortgage required
A buyer who has applied for a high percentage mortgage (say 95% or more) may be unable to proceed if the property is down-valued on survey. Generally speaking buyers who need to borrow a lower percentage of the purchase price are more likely to complete. Cash buyers are the most likely to complete of all.

Choice of lending source
Some lending sources are able to get most mortgage offers out within days. Others take weeks. Ask your estate agent if he has an opinion about the efficiency of the lending source that your buyer has chosen.

Choice of solicitor
A solicitor who is inexperienced, pedantic, overworked or just inefficient can delay a sale for weeks. Ask your agent for his opinion of the firm that the buyer has chosen.

All these factors should be carefully weighed up before you decide on what price you would be prepared to accept from the buyer.

HANDLING AN OFFER FROM A BUYER WHO IS UNABLE TO PROCEED

On many occasions your enquiries will reveal that your would-be buyer is not yet in a position to proceed. Common reasons would be:

- The buyer is unlikely to be able to raise the money.
- The buyer has not yet found a buyer for his own property.
- The buyer has an incomplete chain.

There are very few circumstances where you have anything to gain from giving a commitment to sell your property to someone who is not yet in a position to buy it and the best advice is usually to refuse to even commence negotiations until the buyer is able to proceed. You should be warned that people can get very emotional about losing a house that they have set their heart on and some may try to persuade you to accept their offer by making all sorts of rash promises. Do not be swayed, most will amount to nothing.

When refusing an offer from an unproceedable buyer, the greatest care must be taken to remain on good terms with him. His buying position can and often does change overnight and you must do everything possible to ensure that it is easy for him to come back to you if and when he sells his own property.

SELLING THE BENEFITS OF YOUR POSITION

A good buyer will be just as concerned as you to avoid the expense and disappointment of an abortive sale and the attractiveness of your position as a seller could well influence the price that the buyer is prepared to pay. If you are in a good position to sell, you should be sure to point this out when responding to an offer. Circumstances that may be attractive to a buyer would include:

♦ Able to move out immediately or at short notice if necessary.
♦ Short upward chain.
♦ Not buying another property.
♦ Already found a property to buy.

RESPONDING TO AN OFFER

Your initial response should be in writing. It should follow this format:

1. Thank the purchaser for his offer (regardless of how low it was).

2. Summarise your understanding of the purchaser's buying position (this will help to avoid arguments later).

3. Sell the benefits of your selling position.

4. State the price that you would be prepared to accept.

5. Give your detailed justification for how you arrived at this figure.

6. Restate that you are keen to sell.

7. Ask the buyer to make a revised offer.

Figure 17 is an example of such a letter.

Dear Mr Jones,

Re: 27 The Avenue, Anytown
SUBJECT TO CONTRACT

[1] Thank you for your offer for the above property of £90,000.

[2] I understand that your buying position is as follows:

♦ You have sold your existing property to a first-time buyer.
♦ Your own buyers have a mortgage offer and are pushing you to find somewhere.
♦ You will be arranging a mortgage for approximately 70% of the purchase price from the XYZ Building Society.
♦ You would like to exchange contracts in six to eight weeks.

[3] I confirm that I am not buying another property immediately and that I would be prepared to move out of the house within six to eight weeks.

[4] The price that I would be prepared to accept for the property is £97,000 and I believe that this is fully justified by the prices achieved for similar houses in the area. Relevant comparables include:

Number 37 which has no garage was recently sold for £95,000.
Number 45 which is very similar to mine recently sold for £97,500.

[5] I believe that both the house and my selling position could suit you and your family very well and we would like to sell to you if a price can be agreed. I look forward to hearing from you with a revised offer shortly.

Yours sincerely,

P Smith

Figure 17. Letter responding to an offer.

EMPLOYING NEGOTIATING TECHNIQUES

Few offers will be agreed in the first round. When conducting negotiations it is important to remember that both parties need to feel that they have won. If the other party is allowed to become entrenched in his position, it will become very much more difficult to achieve a satisfactory solution. There are many techniques that can be used to diffuse the hostility of a negotiation.

Ask the purchaser to justify his offer

Almost every estate agent in the country can tell you a story about a sale that fell through because the two parties could not agree about the value of a garden shed, an old piece of carpet, a wooden toilet seat or something equally ridiculous.

The danger of conventional negotiation techniques is that they are highly confrontational. All too often such negotiations become deadlocked because both parties are too proud to concede another round. This is an emotional, not a rational, response but it could easily cost you a sale if you let it.

A much better way to negotiate is based on the simple principle of asking the other party to explain *how* he arrived at his offer. You might achieve this by writing a letter to him along these lines:

Dear Mr Jones,

Re: 27 The Avenue, Anytown.
SUBJECT TO CONTRACT

Thank you for your revised offer of £95,000. In my last letter I showed you how I arrived at my figure of £97,000 by reference to two comparable properties in the immediate area. I wondered if you would be kind enough to let me know how you arrived at your figure of £95,000.

I do hope that we will be able to reach an agreement and I look forward to hearing from you again soon.

Yours sincerely,

P Smith

Figure 18. Letter requesting an explanation of a price offer.

The buyer must respond with some sort of justification for the offer that he has made. This should ensure that future negotiations remain based on factual rather than emotional issues. This technique can be used again and again through subsequent rounds of the negotiations and can play an important role in preventing the negotiations from becoming deadlocked.

Trade concessions for concessions

It can be very dangerous to ask the other party to concede something without giving something in return. You should always be on the lookout for an opportunity to trade a concession for a concession. For example:

◆ If you will pay an extra £1,000 I will agree to take the property off the market immediately.

It is important to realise that the value of the concession need not be equal to the value of what you are asking for in return.

Offering non-financial concessions

A non-cash concession can often have a disproportionate value to the other party. For example, by moving out one day sooner you might be able to save your purchaser from paying a whole month's additional rent. It is therefore well worth trying to find out about any requirements of this nature that your buyer might have. These might include:

◆ completion date
◆ completion periods
◆ exchange date
◆ removal of the property from the market
◆ fixtures and fittings
◆ carpets and curtains.

By making concessions in these areas you might well be able to avoid deadlock and/or secure a valuable negotiating advantage.

Breaking deadlock

It is very frustrating to be unable to agree an offer for the sake of a relatively small amount of money. When the amount at stake is small it can be worth contacting some of the people higher up or down the chain to see if they are prepared to make a contribution. The vendor of a one million pound house at the top of the chain may be prepared to pay a few thousand pounds directly to someone lower down the chain in order to facilitate a move. It is usually best to leave it up to the agent to try to negotiate such a solution.

Always leave the door open

It is surprising how often purchasers who make a low offer for a property early in their search, return to make an acceptable offer for the property days, weeks or even months later. For this reason it is vital to remain on good terms with everyone who makes an offer and to ensure that it is easy for them to reopen negotiations with you at any time in the future.

Consolidation

Once an offer has been agreed, it is important to ensure that all the details are confirmed in writing as soon as possible.

It is also worth trying to arrange to meet your potential purchaser again. A meeting after negotiations have been successfully concluded can play an important role in consolidating the sale. There is no doubt that sales where a personal relationship has been established between the vendor and the purchaser are much more likely to complete.

HANDLING MULTIPLE OFFERS

Occasionally a property will prove to be unexpectedly popular and two or more offers will be made by different purchasers within a short space of time. This can happen for a variety of reasons, one of which is that the property has been marketed at too low a price. If you suspect that this is the case review the comparable evidence before you go any further.

Multiple offers must be handled with great care. It is all too easy to start off with two or three offers and to end up with none. The purpose of this section is to help you to avoid this.

Look at the situation from the purchaser's point of view

Every potential purchaser who tries to buy your property and fails, will be left with a bill for legal and survey fees of several hundred pounds. Each potential purchaser will therefore need to be reassured at the outset that he will be treated fairly and that he has a realistic chance of getting the property. If your behaviour during early negotiations does not achieve this, some or even all of your potential purchasers will withdraw.

Consider all the options

There are seven options for dealing with multiple offers:

1. **A contract race**

   Two or more purchasers are told that whichever of them is able to exchange contracts on the property first will be allowed to buy it.

   Advantages   − no risk to vendor
                         − no need to choose between the parties
                         − more than one chance of selling

   Disadvantages − even the suggestion of a contract race may cause both parties to withdraw
                         − losing party is left with legal fees to pay

2. **Race to mortgage offer**

   Two or more purchasers are told that whoever gets their written mortgage offer first will be allowed to buy the property.

   Advantages   − as above but abortive costs are lower to losing party

   Disadvantages − successful party can still withdraw after mortgage offer received
                         − losing party must still bear some abortive costs
                         − may result in neither party proceeding

3. **Vendor funded contract race (or race to mortgage offer)**

   This works as in option one. However, the vendor agrees to pay the legal and survey costs of whichever party loses up to an agreed figure.

Advantages   – as option one but purchasers more likely to agree to participate if costs are underwritten

Disadvantages – reimbursement of legal fees cannot make up for the disappointment of losing a property
       – suggestion of race may still frighten off both parties
       – cost to vendor will be several hundred pounds

4. Shut out agreement

A legal undertaking is given via the solicitors that one party will be given X weeks to exchange contracts without competition from any other buyer.

Advantages   – seller is protected against a sale dragging on for an unreasonable period

Disadvantages – seller is forced to choose between potential buyers at the outset
       – seller gets no protection against buyer withdrawing

5. Sealed bids

Buyers are invited to submit their best and final offer in writing. The sealed bids are opened at a pre-agreed time and the highest offer wins.

Advantages   – buyers can become excited by a sealed bid contest and overpay
       – system is seen to be fair to all potential buyers

Disadvantages – system has no legal validity and has been discredited by previous unfair competitions in which the opening of the sealed bids has been followed by further rounds of negotiations

– buyer who pays highest price may not be buyer who is most likely to proceed

– a higher price might be obtained by open negotiations

6. Open Negotiations

The agent continues to negotiate with each buyer openly until all but one have dropped out of the bidding.

Advantages – often the best way to obtain the highest price
– purchasers' buying positions can be taken into account

Disadvantages – negotiations can become acrimonious
– successful buyer can withdraw at any time

7. Re-marketing the property

If you feel that the property has been undervalued the only option may be to re-market it. It will usually be necessary to leave a break of several weeks before the property is advertised again. You may also wish to change agents. This will cause considerable delays and when it is re-launched the initial impact will have been spoiled. For these reasons the decision to re-market a property should not be taken lightly.

Deciding which option is best for you

Different options or combinations of options will appeal in different circumstances. If you are selling a highly desirable property in a buoyant market, a contract race may be worth considering. If you are selling an unattractive property during a recession a shut out agreement might be more appropriate. Whatever option you finally choose I would urge you to remember three things:

- Don't rush the decision.
- Take your estate agent's advice.
- Consider each buyer's position as well as the price offered.

Case study

Neville M received an offer of £220,000 for his luxury detached property which was for sale at £249,950. He responded quite aggressively and said that he would not take a penny less that £240,000. Over the next three days negotiations continued until all that was left between them was a garden shed.

The buyer was determined to have it. Neville M felt that he had already conceded so much that he could not bring himself to give in yet again. He eventually told the agent that he would rather burn the shed than let the buyer have it.

The agent offered to pay for a new shed out of his commission but it was too late, negotiations had broken down and the sale did not proceed.

$$\widehat{22}$$

Getting the Sale Through
to Completion

HOW LONG WILL IT TAKE?

Some sales complete within seven days, a few have been
known to complete within 24 hours. However, such
instances are really quite rare. A more usual timescale
for a straightforward sale would be four to eight weeks for
an exchange of contracts and a further four weeks for
completion. A complicated sale could take several times
as long as this.

THE IMPORTANCE OF REGULAR PROGRESS CHASING

Your sale will not complete within the usual timescale
unless you chase it. Some solicitors and mortgage lenders
are like wheelbarrows. If you stop pushing you will come
back to find that they are still exactly where you left them!

You and your agent need to work together to keep the
pressure up. Unfortunately, some agents believe that once
an offer has been accepted, their job is done. You must
make it very clear to your agent that you will not stand for
this. Tell him at the outset that you will expect him to
speak to the purchaser, the lending source and both
solicitors at least once a week until contracts are
exchanged and to report back to you on a weekly basis
with a detailed progress report.

DECIDING WHEN TO TAKE THE PROPERTY OFF THE MARKET

Just because you have accepted an offer, there is nothing to say that you should not continue to market your property. Whether or not to do so can be a difficult decision to make. On the one hand you will wish to show your purchaser good faith. On the other you must remind yourself that a third of all sales don't complete. It may be helpful to delay a final decision on this until after you have done three things:

Double-check the chain

Sometimes in the rush to agree an offer, there is not time to check out the chain in as much detail as you would have liked. If this is the case then the time to get the rest of this background information is now. You cannot give your buyer a commitment to take the property off the market until you are absolutely sure that he is in a position to proceed.

Get to know your purchasers

Consider asking the purchasers to visit you again at home as soon as negotiations have been finalised. The visit will give you an excellent opportunity to make a more accurate assessment of the extent to which you feel you can trust them. It will also give you a chance to get to know each other. The quality of the relationship formed between buyer and seller can be a very important factor in preventing unreasonable behaviour later on.

Consider the alternative options

There are many alternatives to the conventional option of a verbal promise to take the property off the market. Each of the following may be appropriate in different circumstances:

A written lock-out agreement

A very nervous buyer might ask you to sign a lock-out agreement. This is a legal contract that prevents you from selling the property to any other party for a specified period (typically 7–28 days). Such an undertaking should only be given to a buyer who is in an excellent position to proceed and then only as a last resort.

A written or verbal agreement to take the property off the market for a given period (typically 7–28 days)

This gives the buyers a head start but leaves you the option to re-market the property at an early date if their buyer has not made satisfactory progress. Such an undertaking can give considerable comfort to a keen buyer who is in a position to proceed.

Left on market but not advertised

This gives the buyer very little comfort or protection. It may be appropriate in a buoyant market or when there are doubts about the buyer's ability to proceed.

Left on market with an assurance that second offers will not be accepted

The buyer is told that you are not seeking a better offer but that you cannot take the risk of taking the property off the market. This undertaking is virtually worthless and you must be sure that it will not deter a buyer from proceeding. It may be appropriate in a rising market, when you are unsure about the buyer or when you need to hurry the buyer to exchange contracts quickly.

Left on market, no promises
Many good buyers may be unwilling to spend money on survey fees and legal fees when there is no guarantee that they will be able to buy the house. Such a solution is usually only possible in a very buoyant market or with a buyer who is not in a position to proceed.

Whichever option you choose it is vital to keep your word once you have given it. A buyer who is told that a house has been taken off the market will be furious if he sees it advertised the following week. A great many sales fall through because the purchaser is given cause to believe that he cannot trust the vendor to keep his word.

Case study

Stanley and Ethel H agreed a sale on their house within a week of putting it onto the market. They got on well with their buyers and expected the sale to go through without difficulty but just to be on the safe side they decided to leave the property on the market in case anything went wrong. They did not mention this to their buyers.

The following week the buyer rang their agent in a fury. He said that he had just seen the house advertised in the paper – what did Stanley and Ethel think they were playing at? He was doing everything possible to proceed with the sale as quickly as possible. He feared they were trying to obtain a higher offer from another buyer. He said that if that was their attitude he would back out of the sale and buy from someone more trustworthy.

Stanley and Ethel were devastated. It had never been their intention to try to get a higher offer; they just wanted a safety net in case something went wrong.

The agent tried persuading their buyer but to no avail. The house was quickly sold to someone else for the same price but the whole episode left a bad taste and Stanley and Ethel still regret the fact that their buyer accused them unjustifiably of trying to gazump him. With hindsight they wish they had discussed the issue of leaving the property on the market at the very outset.

(22)

Troubleshooting

Most of the problems that are likely to arise during your sale were dealt with in Chapters 11 and 12. However, as a vendor, your objectives will be rather different so in this chapter I will look again at some of the most common problems from the seller's point of view.

INSTRUCTING A SOLICITOR

As a buyer it is desirable to instruct as early as possible in the process. As a vendor it is essential. You should choose your solicitor with care and instruct them the same day that you put your property onto the market. This will enable your solicitor to apply for the Title Deeds, prepare a draft contract and prepare all the other necessary documentation well in advance. This will save at least a fortnight once a buyer is found.

PLANNING AND BUILDING REGULATION PROBLEMS

If you have carried out any major works to your property during your time there, you will need to ensure that you have all the necessary documentation in order. If the building work required planning consent, your solicitor will need a copy of the documentation. If you cannot find it, a copy can be obtained from your local council.

Even if the building work did not require planning permission, it will still need to have building regulation approval, i.e. a certificate from the local council stating that the building work complies with all relevant regulations.

If you do not have such a certificate you must proceed with the utmost caution. Even an informal telephone conversation with the council might trigger an inspection which could result in you being ordered to demolish the extension. Your solicitor will usually be able to advise you regarding the best way forward. In some cases the best solution is to pay an independent architect to check whether the building work complies with regulations. If it does, you can apply for a certificate retrospectively.

If the work does not comply with the regulations, it is often possible for the purchaser to purchase an indemnity policy which would pay them compensation in the event of the council insisting on the demolition of the extension. However, the policy will not pay out if there has been any contact with the council prior to it being issued so you must get professional advice before you do anything.

It is clearly in your best interests to try to ensure that your property is surveyed in the least possible detail. The best way to achieve this is to have available your own recent structural survey. However, if a full structural survey is to take place you should try to ensure that it is combined with the mortgage valuation. Some buyers commission a basic mortgage valuation in the first instance then, once they have the result of this, commission a full structural survey. This is a more expensive way of doing things for the purchaser. Furthermore it can lead to unnecessary delays between the two survey reports.

ADVERSE SURVEY REPORTS

A great many sales fall through because the building society valuer finds defects with the property and/or down-values the property on survey.

Why does it happen?

The valuer is retained by the mortgage lender and his role is to ensure that the property is satisfactory security for the size of the loan that is to be advanced. Because he is retained by the lender, the surveyor will err on the side of caution when valuing a property. The consequence is that the mortgage valuation can often be 5–10% lower than the sale price that has been agreed.

What can be done to pre-empt the problem?

The best way to avoid the problems caused by a down-valuation is to prevent it from happening in the first place. There is a great deal that you can do to achieve this:

1. Choose the lending source

Some banks and building societies have a reputation for using over-cautious valuers. Your estate agent will know which they are, locally. If your purchaser is intending to apply to one of these lending sources, you should ask your agent to try to dissuade them. The best way to do so is by telling them the true reasons for your concerns. If the property is down-valued your buyer will lose his survey fee and have to find another property. He should be as keen to avoid a down-valuation as you and he will often be prepared to reconsider his choice of lending source in order to do so.

2. Choose the surveyor

Some building societies employ their own full-time salaried valuers but most still instruct an independent local surveyor. Each local surveyor will take a different view of property values and most towns have at least one who has a reputation for down-valuing. Your goal must be to prevent this surveyor from valuing your property. Your agent should be able to help you to achieve this by asking the purchaser or his mortgage broker to telephone the building society to request that the particular surveyor is not instructed. They will often comply with such a request.

3. Prepare the house for the survey appointment

Surveyors are human too, and a well-presented house will often be valued at a higher price than an untidy one. You should prepare for the surveyor's appointment in exactly the same way as you would prepare for any other viewing.

4. Show the house to best advantage

The surveyor should be shown around the house in exactly the same way as any other purchaser. First impressions count for a lot and a local surveyor will probably have decided what value to put on the property within a few minutes of arrival.

Once you have shown the surveyor quickly around the house he will wish to be left alone to complete his detailed report. This might take anywhere between 30 minutes and four hours depending on the size of the property and the type of the report that is being prepared.

5. Provide comparable evidence

The surveyor will value your property on the basis of the evidence of prices achieved for similar properties. One of the best ways to protect against a down-valuation is to give the surveyor your own selection of property particulars, chosen to support the sale price achieved for your property. This must be done tactfully. The surveyor will not respond well if he thinks that you are trying to tell him how to do his job.

HANDLING A DOWN-VALUATION

Whatever precautions you take, there is still a very good chance that your property will be down-valued by the surveyor. We will look next at what can be done to limit the damage.

Get in first

Your estate agent will often be able to find out what figure the property has been valued at a day or two before the purchaser is told. This advance warning will enable the agent to present the bad news to the purchasers himself in the right way and can be an important factor in helping him to save the sale.

The initial response

Most buyers will use a surveyor's down-valuation as an excuse to renegotiate the purchase price. You will wish to do everything possible to avoid this happening.

Ask to see the survey report

Before you commence negotiations you should ask for a copy of the survey report. It is in your purchaser's interests to exaggerate the cost and extent of any works that are necessary and purchasers have even been known to invent problems not mentioned by the surveyor in order to try to get a price reduction. You should be very suspicious of a buyer who will not let you see the report. My instinctive reaction would be to refuse to commence negotiations without first seeing a copy of the survey report.

Interpreting the surveyor's report

Dependent upon the urgency of the work, a surveyor will make one of the following recommendations:

♦ He can point out the fault and *recommend* that it is attended to.

♦ He can ask for a *formal undertaking* from the purchasers to carry out the necessary repairs within a certain time.

♦ He can insist that an expert is called in to investigate the extent of the problem and to assess the likely cost of rectifying it.

♦ He can recommend that the mortgage advance be made subject to a *retention*, that is to say that £X000 will be deducted from the mortgage advance and not released until the necessary work has been completed.

♦ He can recommend that the mortgage should be refused altogether.

Handling the renegotiation

Your initial response should be to refuse to renegotiate the price. You might try to defend your position using some of the following arguments:

- The surveyor has been pedantic, the work is not necessary at all.

- The work is of a cosmetic nature. The purchaser did not need a surveyor to point out that the kitchen and bathroom need updating and that the property is in need of redecoration.

- The condition of the property has already been allowed for in the price agreed.

- The other properties recently sold in the area were in a comparable condition.

- The defects mentioned must be seen as fair wear and tear in a property of this age.

Limiting the damage

If renegotiation seems inevitable, there is quite a lot that you can do to limit the damage.

1. **Get your own estimate**
    The surveyor's estimate of the cost of necessary work is likely to be at the top end of the scale. It can be well worth asking a contractor to give an accurate estimate of the cost involved. It could prove to be a lot less than the surveyor thinks.

2. **Offer to carry out the work yourself**
    Very often the buyer has absolutely no intention of carrying out the work that his surveyor has recommended. He is just using the report to get a price reduction. If you suspect that this is the case, you might counter it by offering to do the work yourself between exchange of contracts and completion.

3. **Offer a proportion of the cost**
    If the sale were to fall through at this stage, both
    parties would stand to lose a great deal. Having got so
    far, your buyer will wish to complete the purchase if at
    all possible and may well be prepared to settle for a
    price concession that represents only a small percen-
    tage of the cost of the works.

DEALING WITH A VERY ADVERSE SURVEY

A very adverse survey report would be defined as one
where the mortgage advance is refused altogether or
where a mortgage offer is made subject to a retention of
more than 20% of the property's value. By far the most
common reason for such a result is subsidence.

It is unlikely that you will be able to negotiate your way
out of a situation like this and it is almost inevitable that
you will lose your purchaser and experience considerable
delays before the property can be sold again.

The action you take might include:

1. **Commissioning your own structural survey**
    Just occasionally a second surveyor will not consider
    the problem to be so serious.

2. **Commissioning a specialist structural engineer's report**
    Surveyors have a tendency to spot a crack and assume
    that a property is about to fall down. A structural
    engineer's report might prove that the problem is not
    as severe as it looks.

3. **Making an insurance claim**
   If your property is subsiding, the cost of rectifying this will usually be covered by your buildings insurance.

What to do if negotiations become deadlocked

If negotiations reach deadlock, the best advice would be don't panic and don't give the property away. It is surprising how often a second survey reveals none of the problems mentioned in the first.

GAZUMPING

The practice of gazumping arouses fierce passions. It happens when the vendor agrees a sale for his property and then subsequently accepts a higher offer from another party. It can happen at any time during the sales process, from five minutes after the first offer was accepted right up to the day that exchange of contracts was due to take place.

Whose fault is it?

Gazumping is caused by human greed, not by estate agents. An estate agent's professional and legal duty is to carry out the instructions of his client. If his client instructs him to continue marketing a property after an offer has been accepted, then he must do so. If a second offer is subsequently received, it is the agent's legal duty to pass the offer on to the vendor. It is entirely up to the vendor to decide whether to accept or refuse the higher price.

If you receive a higher offer after you have agreed a sale, you need to proceed very carefully. It is all too easy to start with two offers and end up with none at all.

Check out the second buyer's position

Before you do anything you must check out that the second buyer is in a position to proceed. Having checked out his position, compare it with the current position of your original buyer. At one extreme there would be nothing to gain from accepting an offer that was only marginally higher from a purchaser who has not yet sold his own property. At the other extreme it would be much harder to turn down a higher offer from a cash buyer the day after your original purchaser has lost the buyer for his own property.

Assess the value of all other factors

You must also be sure to weigh up the value of all other relevant factors in the equation. These might include:

1. **Timescale**
   How quickly could the second purchaser complete? Would this delay cost you money (e.g. in extra mortgage payments)?

2. **Fairness of price**
   Is your property really worth the high price? If it is not the second sale may well not complete due to a down-valuation on survey.

3. **Risk of losing your purchase**
   Would the delay caused by switching buyers jeopardise your own purchase?

Consider all the options

There are many alternative ways in which you can use a second offer to your advantage. The options include:

- Accept the second offer and tell the original buyer they have lost the property.

- Inform the original buyers that you have received a higher offer from another party and invite them to match it. (This might go more than one round before a new price is finally agreed.)

- Invite both parties to compete in a contract race for the property. (Benefit: quicker completion.)

- Inform the original buyers that you have received a second offer. Tell them that you will not accept it provided that they exchange contracts before a certain date. (Benefit: quicker completion.)

- Inform the original buyer that you have received a second offer which you will not accept because you have agreed to sell it to them. (Benefit: consolidates relationship with original buyer but implies that competition is on the horizon.)

- Refuse second offer; don't tell the original buyer that you received one (This is sometimes the best way to deal with a nervous buyer.)

Moral and ethical considerations

This section would not be complete without a few words about the effects of gazumping on the purchaser. If you do accept a second offer, the original buyers will be left with a substantial bill for abortive survey fees and legal costs in addition to the disappointment of having lost the property that they had set their hearts on. It is not my place to attempt to define the limits of moral behaviour, but I would ask that you should at least pause to consider the consequences of your actions, before you make your final decision.

GAZUNDERING

When the market is poor gazundering is a common problem. A vendor is 'gazundered' when the buyer reduces his offer, without good reason, shortly before exchange of contracts is due to take place.

The buyer who tries this tactic is banking on the fact that the financial and emotional costs to you of pulling out of the sale at such a late stage, will exceed the value of the reduction that he has asked for. When the property market is poor, buyers often get away with it. The following suggestions will help you to limit the damage if your purchaser tries to gazunder you:

1. **Negotiate via the agent**
    You will probably be very angry with the buyer for trying to gazunder you and this anger will seriously reduce your ability to negotiate effectively. Further negotiations really must therefore be conducted via the estate agent.

2. **Ask for reasons**
    Ask the buyer why he has reduced his offer at such a late stage. The buyer's embarrassment about the situation will be increased if he is forced to admit that he has no reason to ask for a price reduction and that he's just trying it on.

3. **Rejustify the price**
   Use comparable evidence to justify that the property is worth the original price that was agreed.

The final decision
If these tactics don't work you will be forced to make a decision about whether to accept the reduced offer. It is all too easy to allow anger and emotion to get in the way of making the right decision. Before you tell your purchaser to go to hell, be sure to weigh up the financial value of factors such as:

◆ Extra mortgage payments whilst the property is remarketed.

◆ The financial and emotional cost of losing your purchase.

◆ Your realistic chances of obtaining the same price again from another purchaser.

If you have a reserve buyer waiting in the wings you might be in a position to call your purchaser's bluff but on many other occasions the best thing to do is to bite your lip and accept the lower offer.

Dealing with the consequences
There are two things that you might wish to do to claw back some of the money that you have had to concede to your purchaser.

1. **Gazunder your own vendor**
   Telephone the agent that you are buying through, explain that you have been gazundered and say that

you fear that you will not now be able to complete your purchase at the original price agreed. This is a high-risk strategy. You may lose your purchase altogether, but if market conditions are so bad that you felt compelled to accept a lower offer, then your vendor might be forced to do the same.

2. **Remove fixtures and fittings**
   If all else has failed you might consider getting your own back by removing all fixtures and fittings not included in the contract. These might include things such as extra security locks, bathroom fitments, shelves, light fittings, plants, etc. The collective value of these fittings can often run to many hundreds or even thousands of pounds.

IF THE BUYER WITHDRAWS

Try to establish the reason

My experience is that once a buyer says that he wishes to withdraw from the purchase he usually does so. However, before you completely give up on your purchaser, it is worth double-checking to make sure that you know the real reason for his change of heart. It is surprisingly common to find that there are problems that you don't know about which might be solvable. For example, your buyer might have been refused a mortgage and be too embarrassed to tell the agent this. Instead he just says that he has changed his mind. If the agent can find out the truth, he might be able to help him to obtain a loan from another lending source.

Don't despair
However disappointed you are, try not to despair. Your property sold once and it will sell again, you just need to be patient.

Don't proceed with your purchase
Unless you are extremely wealthy, you should not even think about continuing with your purchase until you have found a buyer for your own property. One of the saddest cases that I dealt with as an agent involved a family who took out a ruinously expensive bridging loan to buy their dream home, failed to sell their previous home and ended up having both repossessed by the mortgage lenders. It could easily happen to you. However perfect your dream home is there will always be another.

DEALING WITH CHAINS
All the problems that I have covered in this section can also occur with other sales up or down the chain. If you suspect that your own sale is being jeopardised or delayed by the inexperience or pigheadedness of other buyers and sellers in the chain, you may need to take matters into your own hands.

Establishing what the problem is
It can be surprisingly difficult to find out the real cause of the delay. As in the game of Chinese Whispers, information tends to be distorted when it is passed through the many parties involved in the chain. Furthermore, once tempers have be frayed, many parties seem to become more interested in whose fault it is that the chain is being held up, than in finding a way in which the problem can be resolved. You will need to work hard to cut through such nonsense.

Start with your estate agent

It is your agent's job to know what is happening up and down the chain and he should certainly have an opinion as to what is causing the delay. However, no matter how convincing his explanation sounds, don't take his word for it. Ask him to contact all the other agents up and down the chain in order to establish the up-to-date position with each sale from first-hand sources.

Checking a chain via the solicitors

If you are still not satisfied with the answers you are getting, a second option is to try to track the sale through the solicitors. Conveyancing solicitors habitually blame the other side for all delays, so ignore any such allegations and concentrate your questions on establishing where the problems lie and whether there is anything that you can do to expedite matters.

Start by asking your solicitor for his opinion as to where the problem lies. You might then consider checking this by phoning some or all of the solicitors in the chain. They are under no obligation to talk to you, and some will refuse to do so, but most will give you five minutes at least which should be ample time for you to achieve your purpose.

Checking discreetly with other vendors

A final option is to try to speak directly to all the other parties in the chain. Each vendor will almost certainly be able to give you a telephone number for his own purchaser and in this way it should be possible for you to speak personally to everyone involved.

You will probably be surprised by the number of contradictory stories that you hear from different parties. The only safe way to be sure that you have established the real problem is to obtain information from several different sources so that you may cross check its accuracy.

Late survey/mortgage denied
If a buyer further down the chain is having problems obtaining a mortgage then there is a great deal that you might be able to do to help. Better still send them a copy of this book open at the relevant page!

Inefficient solicitors
A less informed buyer in the chain might have instructed a solicitor who is inexperienced, overworked, lazy, pedantic or just downright bloody-minded.

The best person to help you to overcome the shortcomings of another solicitor in the chain is your own solicitor. If you are faced with this situation you should ring your own solicitor and share your concerns with him. In return for payment for the extra time involved he might be able to guide, cajole or bully the other solicitor into doing the job that he is being paid for.

Down-valuation on survey or gazundering
The recommendations made earlier may help to diffuse the situation. If negotiations have already reached dead-lock you might consider trying three last things.

1. **Offer to mediate**
    You might offer to act as a mediator for one final round of negotiation. If previous negotiations have

been handled clumsily, you might still be able to snatch victory from the jaws of defeat.

2. **'Pass the hat up the chain'**
   Other parties in the chain might be prepared to contribute a sum of money to resolve a problem. This will often cost you less than the cost of an abortive sale. This hypothetical example shows a situation when such an offer benefits all parties:

   Property 1 sale price £50,000
   Property 2 sale price £100,000
   Property 3 sale price £150,000
   Property 4 sale price £250,000
   Property 5 sale price £500,000 (vendors moving into newly built retirement home)

   A down-valuation of 10% on Property 1 would leave the buyers £5,000 short of the funds needed to complete. To a first-time buyer this would be a great deal of money. The vendors of Property 1 could not afford to concede £5,000 and the sale would fall through. However, the vendor of Property 5 could easily afford to fund the £5,000 shortfall, and it might well be in his best financial interests to do so. £5,000 represents approximately two months' loss of interest on the proceeds or one month's interest on a £500,000 mortgage.

3. **Make a personal contribution**
   An alternative solution might be for the vendors of Properties 3, 4 and 5 to agree to contribute £1,000, £1,000 and £3,000 respectively. This would represent

approximately one month's extra mortgage for each of them.

It is surprising how often an insoluble problem can be overcome by passing the hat up the chain this way. All that is needed is someone with the knowledge and determination to negotiate it. In the absence of a better offer that someone will have to be you.

As an absolute last resort you might even consider offering to pay the disputed sum yourself either alone or in conjunction with other parties in the chain.

IF THE CHAIN BREAKS DOWN
The suggestions given in the last chapter may help you to save a sale at the eleventh hour but realistically you must accept that in many cases you will be unsuccessful.

If the chain does break down, there are two last things that you might try to save the day.

Subsidise a sale lower down the chain
This is essentially a variation on passing the hat up the chain. Consider this example.

Property 1 was sold at £50,000 to first-time buyer
Property 2 was sold at £100,000
Property 3 was sold at £150,000
Property 4 was sold at £250,000
Property 5 was sold at £500,000 (the vendor was elderly and was not buying another property)

Two days before contracts were due to be exchanged the buyer of the £50,000 property withdrew for no reason.

The solution which was agreed worked as follows:

Each vendor contributed 1% of their sale price to a communal fund thus:

Vendor 1 contributed	£500
Vendor 2 contributed	£1,000
Vendor 3 contributed	£1,500
Vendor 4 contributed	£2,500
Vendor 5 contributed	£5,000
Total	£10,000

This money was used to subsidise the selling price of the £50,000 property. Thus it was put back on the market at the bargain price of £40,000. As a result it sold within hours and the chain was saved.

Sadly solutions like this rarely work because the parties let their emotions get in the way of finding a solution or because no one available has the skill, patience, motivation and tenacity to negotiate a solution that is acceptable to everybody.

Consider a part exchange
One last extreme solution to consider, if all else failed, is to offer to buy the property that is holding up your sale as a part exchange. If you have the funds available it is not as daft an idea as it sounds. Reconsider our previous example. The vendor of a property selling at £500,000 and not buying again would stand to lose a lot from a delay of three to four months whilst his property is re-marketed. At say 6% per annum, loss of interest alone

comes to £2,500 per month. It might well pay a person in this position to buy a cheap property in part exchange in order to expedite his own sale. Loss of interest on a £50,000 flat would, after all, be only £250 per month. The cost of buying and reselling the flat would be around £2,000. It is easy to see how the vendor could be better off. You should at least check the sums relating to your own position on the back of an envelope before you dismiss the idea out of hand.

MAKING YOURSELF HOMELESS

All the things that could go wrong further down the chain can also go wrong with transactions further up it. However, there is one further factor to consider if you have lost or are at risk of losing your purchase and that is whether you should still complete on your own sale. The arguments for and against doing so are often finely balanced. Facts to consider include:

1. **State of the market**
   If you are moving to a more expensive property in a buoyant market there is a risk that prices will continue to rise whilst you are out of the market. If the market is depressed you may be able to buy the next property for less than you had anticipated.

2. **Improved negotiating position**
   Without a property to sell you will be in a much stronger buying position. This may enable you to negotiate to buy your next property at a much better price.

3. **Cost of storage and removals**

   The cost of removals to and from your temporary address and/or storage charges will be quite significant.

4. **Non-financial factors**

   Moving house is extremely disruptive. You must be sure to include the emotional cost of an extra move on both yourself and your family.

Taking all these factors into account it is probably not surprising that most vendors who lose their purchase would rather run the risk of losing their own buyer than face a double move.

Case study

Aaron and Dorothy C agreed a sale of their Victorian property at a figure of £120,000. Their buyer's surveyor found a number of defects with the property including 'a roof that would need replacing within five years' and faults with the damp course. The surveyor said in this condition the property was worth only £105,000.

Aaron and Dorothy were not prepared to sell at this price and the buyer withdrew. A second sale was agreed also at £120,000 and a second survey arranged with a different surveyor. The problems with the damp course came up again but the roof was not mentioned and this time the surveyor's valuation was £115,000.

Aaron and Dorothy obtained an estimate that showed that the cost of rectifying the damp course was less than the surveyors had estimated and on this basis the sale went through at a price of £117,000.

Commenting on their experience Aaron and Dorothy said 'I'm so glad we didn't sell to the first buyer at £105,000. It just shows that surveyors' opinions and valuations can vary considerably.'

Case study

Stephen and Irene Y agreed a sale at £100,000 on their three-bedroom detached property. They were buying a four-bedroom property at £150,000 and were in some hurry to find a buyer.

They left their property on the market 'just in case something went wrong with the original sale'. A week later they received a second offer for their property of £105,000. After some discussion they decided to take it. Their original buyer was furious but there was nothing that he could do about it.

Unfortunately the vendors of the house that Stephen and Irene were buying found out that their original sale had 'fallen through'. They said they could not wait any longer and sold to someone else. Stephen and Irene continued with their sale at £105,000. However, the property was down-valued on survey to £100,000 and this was the price they were forced to accept.

Furthermore the only four-bedroom detached house available on the estate that they wanted to move to was for sale at £160,000 and they had to agree an offer of £158,000 to get it.

Commenting on their experiences Stephen and Irene said 'With hindsight we should have stayed with our original buyers. We would have been £8,000 better off and we would have had the peace of mind of having behaved in a more ethical way'.

(23)

Home Buying in the Future

The present home-buying process leaves much to be desired. It is slow, bureaucratic and expensive. Worst of all, one third of all sales break down before exchange of contracts, causing untold stress, disappointment and expense to hundreds of thousands of people every year.

In December 1998 the Government published a consultation paper which proposed radical changes to the house-buying process. Its proposal was that new legislation should be introduced which would make it a *criminal* offence for anyone to market a property without first preparing a seller's information pack. For freehold properties this information pack would include:

♦ Copies of title documents.

♦ Replies to standard preliminary enquiries made on behalf of buyers.

♦ Replies to local authority searches.

♦ Copies of any planning, listed building and building regulations consents.

♦ For new properties, copies of warranties and guarantees.

♦ Any guarantees for work carried out on the property

♦ A surveyor's report on the condition of the property.

For leasehold properties the pack would also include:

◆ A copy of the lease.

◆ Accounts and receipts for service charges.

◆ Building insurance policy and receipts for premiums.

◆ Regulations made by the landlord or management company.

◆ The landlord or management company's memorandum and articles.

The cost of producing this pack will be approximately £500–700 for the typical property. This would have to be borne by the vendor *before* they could put their property onto the market.

If introduced the consequence of this legislation would be very far reaching:

◆ In future buyers may be able to exchange contracts on the spot. At the moment it takes around eight weeks.

◆ In future, costs would be borne by the seller. At the moment they are borne by the purchaser.

◆ In future all legal work would be completed before the house is put onto the market. At the moment it is not done until after a buyer has been found.

This legislation was originally going to be introduced in January 2003. However, in light of considerable opposition from both property professionals and a Parliamentary Select Committee, the legislation has been postponed until at least January 2006.

Most property professionals agree that the relevant legal documentation should be prepared before a property is put onto the market. However, there is deep resistance to the idea of compelling vendors to commission their own survey.

The problem with the current proposal is that purchasers will not be able to use this survey report for mortgage valuation purposes. Consequently, purchasers will have to pay for a separate survey to be carried out on the same property. This is absurd.

If this legislation is introduced in its current form, my prediction would be that the dual survey problem will quickly be resolved by market forces. A mortgage lender will say they will not require a second survey for mortgage valuation purposes provided that the loan is less than 75% of the property's value. Another lender will say that they will not require a survey if the loan is less than 80% of the property's value. Before long the requirement for a second valuation for mortgage purposes will be dropped altogether.

Instead mortgage lenders will protect their interests by relying upon their increasingly sophisticated credit scoring procedures to ensure that the mortgagee is creditworthy. They will also carry out an approximate valuation of the property on line by checking the sale price against the prices achieved for other properties sold in the immediate area. This data is now available on line from the Land Registry.

However, there is a good chance that the legislation will not be introduced at all. What might happen instead is that forward-thinking estate agents, surveyors and solicitors might implement the best ideas from the legislation voluntarily in order to gain a commercial advantage. If enough companies do so, the legislation might become unnecessary. This would be an excellent outcome and there is considerable evidence to show that it is already starting to happen:

◆ A lot of estate agents are now encouraging their vendors to instruct solicitors the same day that they put their property onto the market. This saves two weeks in a typical sale.

◆ A lot of the more forward-thinking solicitors are now offering a 'no sale no fee' guarantee. This means that house sellers can now instruct a solicitor to prepare all the necessary documentation without financial risk.

◆ Modern technology has reduced considerably the amount of time it takes for lenders to process a mortgage application. In fact one major lender is just about to launch an on line application service that will allow applicants to obtain an unconditional mortgage offer within an hour. If this is successful you can be sure that other lenders will quickly follow.

Perhaps in a few years time it really will be possible to view a house in the morning and move in the same afternoon!

As soon as the new home-buying process has been resolved we will bring out a new edition of this book. In the meanwhile, I hope that this current edition will help you to avoid the worst pitfalls in the current system.

The Last Word

Moving house will never be easy, but I hope that this book has helped you to avoid some of the common pitfalls. All that remains now is to enjoy your new home.

And this book. Well this book might serve one last useful purpose. I would suggest that you put it on a bookshelf in a prominent position so that if, at any time in the future, you find yourself thinking – 'Wouldn't it be nice to have an extra bedroom' – you can look at the cover and ask yourself – is it really worth it?

Glossary

Estate agents use a great many technical terms which can be very confusing at first. The following are some of the most common.

AGENTS' TERMS

Applicant A potential purchaser enquiring for a property to buy.

Company move A term used to describe a move with financial assistance from employers.

Corporate estate agents A term used to describe the firms of estate agents which are owned by the financial institutions.

Dependent sale A term used to describe a sale to a purchaser who has to sell their property before being in a financial position to proceed.

Disinstruction A vendor advises they no longer wish their property to be offered for sale.

Financial consultant Somebody who is qualified under the Financial Services Act to give financial advice.

Financial services An umbrella term used to describe mortgage arrangements and insurance policies which are offered to clients and customers.

Gazumping A term used when a vendor accepts a higher offer after agreeing a sale with a purchaser subject to contract.

Gazundering A term that is used when a purchaser reduces the offer that they have made for a property at the very last moment.

Independent estate agents A term used to describe the estate agency firms which are still owned by private individuals or companies that are not linked to a financial institution.

Joint sole agency A term used to describe an agency where two or more agents agree to share the commission regardless of which of them achieves the sale.

Lettings A term used to describe the renting rather than the selling of property.

Listing A term used to describe property that has been taken onto the market for sale.

Mortgage valuation A valuation for the lender of mortgage finance.

Multiple agency A term used to describe the situation where two or more agents are instructed to sell a property on terms where the first agent to achieve a sale will earn the entire commission.

No chain A sale where the vendor and purchaser are not buying or selling other properties.

Personal interest An estate agent is not allowed to purchase a property that his/her employer is selling without declaring a personal interest to the vendors. Agents must also declare a personal interest when they are selling a property which they own through the firm that employs them.

PMA An abbreviation for the Property Misdescriptions Act.

Relocation A term used to describe moving to a different part of the country with financial assistance from the employers.

Repossession A property that has been repossessed by the mortgagees due to the non-payment of the mortgage.

Retention A sum of money which is held back by a mortgage lender until certain specified works have been completed to a required standard.

Sole agency The term used to describe an agent who is appointed as the only agent who will be offering a property for sale during a given period (see statutory definition).

Survey A visit to a property by a surveyor who will compile a report on the structural condition and/or value of a property.

Take-on A property that has been taken onto the market for sale.

Touting A direct approach to the vendors of properties which are being offered for sale by another estate agent (NB: the NAEA have specific rules governing this).

Under offer An alternative term for a property that is sold subject to contract.

Vacant possession A property which will be vacant on completion day.

Valuation An estate agent's visit to value a house with a view to putting the property on the market.

Vendor The person who is selling a property.

LEGAL TERMS

Contract A legal document setting out the terms under which a sale will take place.

Covenant A restriction on the use of a freehold property (e.g. it must be used for residential purposes only).

Deeds The legal documents that prove ownership of a property.

Exchange of contracts The point at which the sale usually becomes binding.

Flying freehold A freehold property, all or part of which is supported by another adjoining property as opposed to being connected to the ground.

Freehold A property which is owned in perpetuity.

Leasehold A property that the owner will only be able to use for certain term. Many leases are originally granted for 99 years. At the end of this time ownership of the property will revert to the freeholder.

Legal completion The day upon which money is paid and the purchaser usually has the right to occupy the property.

Legal executive Somebody who works for a legal firm undertaking legal work but is not a qualified solicitor.

Licensed conveyancer Somebody other than a solicitor who is licensed to undertake conveyancing work.

Memorandum of sale A summary of the main Terms and Conditions for a sale which is sent out to the vendor, purchaser and both solicitors when a sale is first agreed.

Mortgage indemnity An insurance policy which protects a lender from incurring financial loss in the event that a property is sold for less than the mortgage that is secured on it.

Mortgage offer A binding promise by a mortgage lender to lend money to a purchaser of a property usually with conditions.

Mortgage retention When the property requires work the mortgage lender will occasionally retain a portion of the mortgage funds until such time as that work has been completed to their satisfaction.

Outline planning The local authority has given approval for an outline scheme which is then followed by detailed proposals.

Planning permission Permission granted by the local council for development or a change of use to a property.

Policy An insurance policy which covers a mortgage lender against losses that might be incurred in the event that a property is sold for a price that is lower than the amount of the mortgage that is outstanding.

Probate sale A term used to describe the sale of a property where the owner is deceased.

Repayment A conventional type of mortgage where money is borrowed and repaid with interest over the full term.

Search An enquiry that is made of the local authority to check that nothing adverse is likely to happen in the immediate vicinity (such as a new road scheme).

Sold subject to contract An offer has been accepted but exchange of contracts has not taken place.

Solicitor Somebody who is qualified by the Law Society to give legal advice.

PROPERTY TERMS

Air bricks Bricks with ventilation holes in them to allow air to circulate beneath the floors of a building.

Annexe A self-contained portion of a large house. An annexe is often used to house an elderly relative.

Bay fronted A property where the windows protrude from the front wall of the property.

Block insurance A type of building insurance policy which covers all the flats in a building.

Box bay A bay window built in an oblong shape with two 90 degree corners.

Bungalow A single storey dwelling.

Canopy porch A porch comprising of a roof only with open sides.

Capped chimney A chimney which has been sealed at the top to prevent the entry of birds and/or dampness.

Casement window Type of window which is hinged at the top, side or bottom.

Cavity walls A form of construction whereby two brick walls are built with a small space between them. This form of construction provides much better stability and weather protection.

Chalet bungalow A bungalow with some first-floor rooms built under the slope of the roof.

Cylinder lock A lock which can be opened from the inside without a key (e.g. a Yale lock).

Detached A house which is not joined to any other building on any side.

Dormer window A type of window which protrudes from a pitched roof allowing the glass to be held in a vertical position.

Double bay A property with two bay windows.

Double garage A garage where two cars can be parked side by side.

Double glazing Two layers of glass held in place by a single frame usually with the purpose of reducing heat loss through the windows.

En-suite bathroom A bathroom for the sole use of a bedroom and with a door that connects directly to it.

Ex-council A house that was originally built for rent by the local authority.

Fitted wardrobes A wardrobe which is built in as part of the property.

Flat A self-contained portion of a building with its own kitchen and bathroom facilities.

Flat roof A horizontal roof often covered in felt which requires regular renewal.

Gable The triangular shaped vertical portion of wall at the end of the roof.

Gas radiator central heating A gas boiler which heats a property with panel radiators through which flow hot water.

Gas warm air A type of heating system where a gas boiler is used to heat air which is circulated through ducts to each room of the property with the assistance of an electrical fan.

Ground rent An annual rental made to the freeholder under the terms of a long lease.

Hard standing A cement or tarmac area designed for the parking of a motor vehicle.

House insurance Another term for building insurance which covers the owner of the property.

Integral garage A garage which is built within the walls of the main property and could have access to the property via an integral door.

Leaded light The small panes of glass often seen in cottage windows.

Link detached A detached house with an attached garage which is attached to another adjoining building.

Loft conversion A term used to describe a room or rooms which have been formed in what was originally the roof space.

Maisonette A flat with its own front door which has access direct to the outside opposed to via a communal hall way, or a two or more storey flat.

Mortice lock A lock which cannot be opened from either side without a key and is set within the body of the door.

Oil-fired central heating Central heating which is powered by an oil burning boiler.

Open-plan A house with no internal walls to separate the living room, the dining room and the kitchen.

Open fireplace A fireplace which is designed for use with a coal or log fire.

Pitched roof The traditional style of roof pitched at an angle and usually covered in slate or tiles.

Purlin One of the timbers supporting a pitched roof. A purlin is the timber that supports the rafters to stop sagging.

Quarter back A group of houses built in a square with two outside walls and two walls shared with the adjoining properties.

Reception room An old-fashioned term to describe the main living rooms.

Render A sand and cement coating applied to the external wall of a property and often painted or textured.

Roof trusses The larger triangulated structures usually built of timber which support the main weight of the roof.

RSJ A steel beam which supports the weight of a structure over an opening.

Sash windows The type of window which slides vertically up and downwards.

Secondary glazing Two layers of glass held in place by two separate frames with the purpose of reducing either heat loss or improving sound insulation on a window.

Shared driveway A driveway which is shared with one or more other properties.

Single skin extension An extension with a wall constructed of a single layer of brick (4.5in. thick). Such extensions are usually not suitable for permanent habitation.

Single storey extension A single storey extension built onto a property.

Skylight windows A window which is at the same angle as the pitched roof itself.

Split level A house where each storey is built on more than one level. Such houses are usually built on a hillside.

Stone cladding A thin layer of stone or imitation stone which is attached to the external wall of a property

Storage heater A type of electric heating which heats up usually using cheap electricity available at night and discharges this heat throughout the day.

Stud wall An internal wall made from a wooden frame rather than brick.

Studio A type of small flat comprising one room which is used for living, sleeping and cooking together with a separate bathroom.

Tandem garage A double-length garage where two vehicles are parked one behind the other.

Terraced house A house that is joined to the adjoining buildings on both sides.

Thatched roof A roof which is covered with straw or reeds rather than tiles.

Tile hung Tiles hung on a vertical wall either for decorative purposes or to keep out dampness.

Timber frame construction A form of construction where the building is based around a timber frame taking the load.

Timber treatment Any treatment to the timber in a property, e.g. woodworm, dry rot or wet rot.

Town house A three or four storey house with integral garage occupying the ground floor. Usually found in town centre locations where living space and parking space is at a premium and usually in a terrace.

Traditional construction The traditional form of building where the external walls of the property are load bearing and of masonry construction.

UPVC An abbreviation for a particular type of plastic window frame.

Wall tie A metal tie that connects the inner and outer sections of a cavity wall in order to improve the structural stability.

TECHNICAL TERMS

Contents insurance An insurance policy that protects a householder in the event of their furniture or other contents being lost, damaged or stolen.

Detailed planning permission The permission for development according to detailed planning specifications.

Dot screen photo A special type of photograph designed for clear reproduction on a photocopier.

Dry rot A type of fungus which can cause serious damage to a building.

Endowment A type of combined savings and life assurance policy often sold as a vehicle to repay a mortgage at a future date with interest only being paid during the term.

Fixtures and fittings A collective term that is applied to any removable fixtures or fittings which may or may not be included in the sale price.

Penetrating damp Dampness that is penetrating through the walls, usually as a result of a defect such as a crack or perhaps a leaking drainpipe.

Re-pointing The restoration of the mortar between the bricks on an external wall.

Rising damp Dampness which is transmitted up from the ground due to the failure or absence of a damp course.

Septic tank A method of disposing of sewage when a property is not connected to a main sewer.

Structural engineer's report A specialist report on a property where there is evidence of structural movement or a potential risk.

Structural survey A comprehensive survey which reports in detail on the condition of a property.

Subsidence Structural damage caused to a property due to its sinking into the ground.

Wet rot Wood that has rotted because of it being saturated by damp.

Useful Addresses

British Association of Removers, 3 Churchill Court, 58 Station Road, North Harrow HA2 7SA. Tel: 020 8861 3331. www.bar.co.uk

National Association of Conveyancers, 2–4 Chichester Rents, Chancery Lane, London WC2A 1EG. Tel: 020 7404 5737

The Law Society, 113 Chancery Lane, London WC2A 1EL. Tel: 020 7242 1222. www.lawsoc.org.uk

The Law Society of Scotland, PO Box 75, 26 Drumsheugh Gardens, Edinburgh EH3 7YR. Tel: 0131 226 7411. www.lawscot.co.uk

The National Association of Estate Agents, Arbon House, 21 Jury Street, Warwick CV34 4EH. Tel: 01926 496800. www.naea.co.uk

The Royal Institution of Chartered Surveyors, 12 Great George Street, Parliament Square, London SW1P 3AD. Tel: 020 7222 7000. www.rics.org

Internet addresses

asserta.co.uk

Fish4.co.uk

Primelocation.com

propertyfinder.co.uk

rightmove.com

Vebra.com

Index

accompanied viewings, 237
adverse surveys, 286
advertising, 185, 188, 231

boundary disputes, 148
bridging loans, 31
building regulations, 151, 279
building surveyors, 14
buying agents, 8

capital growth, 4
cashback mortgages, 5
chain checking, 293
charges certificate, 17
commission disputes, 253
comparables, 82
completion dates, 153
compulsory insurances, 51
conditional offers, 28
connected services, 221
contract races, 269
conveyancing process, 24, 25
County Court Judgements

for debts (CCJs), 37
credit scoring, 35

damp proof course, 18
damp reports, 18, 138
deed of variation, 155
defective leases, 154
deposits, 8
disinstructing an agent, 252
dogs, 238
down-valuations, 131, 283
draft contracts, 14
dry rot, 17

editorial, 235
employment references, 38
endowment mortgages, 54
engrossed contracts, 19
exchange of contracts, 159

fee negotiation, 24
final searches, 161
fixed rate mortgages, 47
fixtures and fittings, 152